The PennyWhistle™
HALLOWEEN
BOOK

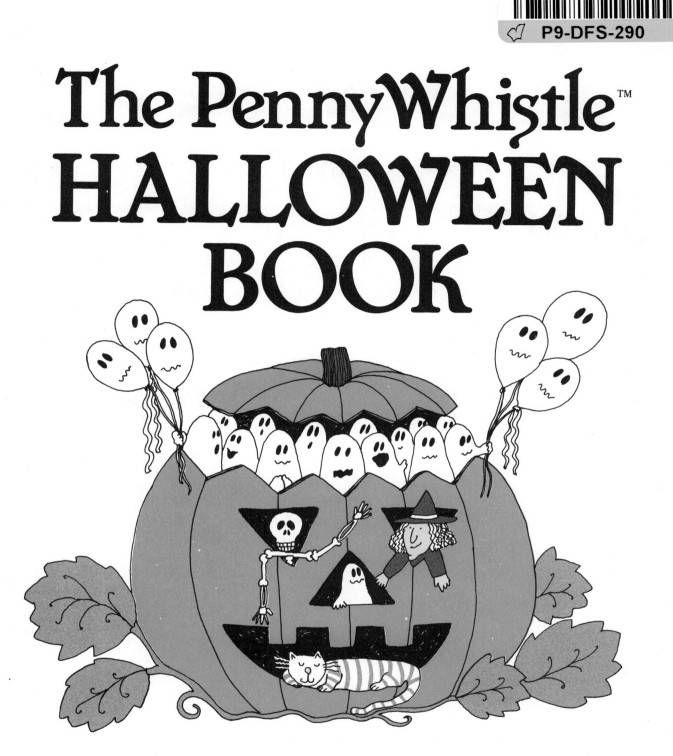

Meredith Brokaw & Annie Gilbar

DESIGNED & ILLUSTRATED BY JILL WEBER

F

A FIRESIDE BOOK
Published by Simon & Schuster
New York London Toronto Sydney Tokyo Singapore

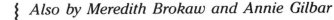

Also by Meredith Brokaw and Annie Gilbar

THE PENNY WHISTLE™ PARTY PLANNER
THE PENNY WHISTLE™ LUNCH BOX BOOK

F

FIRESIDE
Simon & Schuster Building
Rockefeller Center
1230 Avenue of the Americas
New York, New York 10020

First Fireside Edition 1991
Published by arrangement with the authors.

FIRESIDE and colophon are registered trademarks of Simon & Schuster Inc.

Designed by Jill Weber
Manufactured in the United States of America

10 9 8 7 6 5 4 3   Pbk.

ISBN 0-671-73791-0 Pbk.

Penny Whistle Toys is a registered trademark of Penny Whistle Toys, Inc. and is used
herein by permission.

TO
DAN GREEN

Who knew Halloween was right,
But doesn't know we always knew—
Behind his curmudgeon costume
Lies a gentle genius.

THANK YOU, THANK YOU, THANK YOU, to the friends
who shared their stories, recipes, and lovely, lively ideas. Happy
Halloween to all!

Heather Auld
Allen Beekman
Pam Belknapp
Rebecca Bloom
Joyce Bogart
Barbara Harvey Brandenburgh
Sarah, Jennifer & Andrea Brokaw
Iris Brooks
The Buhai Family
Carol Chalmers (The Toy Store)
Harvey & Jean Cotter
Tom & Marcia Curley
Molly Damm
Dr. Dean Donaldson
Bob & Patty Dorf
Marian & Howard Downs
Trisha & Lindsay Feldman
Ray Gaulke
Lisa & Marc Gilbar
Ariana, Rob & Bobbi Gordon
Ronna Gordon
Peter Gordon
Lynda Guber
Inadoll Harvey
Nancy Harakay
Andrea Hirshhorn
Karen Holland (The Wooden Horse)
Gerri Karetsky

Leslie Larson
Wes Laseski
Larry Liff (Imagineering)
Mary Macucci
Josh Mann
Richard Mann
John McKiernan (Miller Toys)
Patricia Messina
Keita Metz
Pam Morris
Dana Nye (The Ben Nye Company)
Kay O'Connell
Bob & Sandy Pittman
J.J. Ramberg
Bill Roser (The Wooden Swing)
Annie Rusoff
Dr. Lee Salk
Judy Schadlich
Joanna Seitz
Barry Shapiro
Obie & Joey Slamon
Mary Slawson
Bud Trillin
Maggie Moss Tucker
Daryl Weill
Lainie Witherspoon
Tracy Zabar

ALWAYS, to Jill Weber, Kathy Robbins, Pam Lyons, Betty Lee,
Harriet Ripinsky, and, of course, Gary Gilbar and Tom Brokaw.

CONTENTS

The Story of Halloween

Myths and Mirths: If the Druids Could See Us Now!

The night is somber, gloomy, and overcast. The atmosphere is still and ominous. The moon is partially hidden by threatening clouds. There are odd sounds. The first is a seemingly innocent meow of a black cat, silhouetted against that eerie moon. Then there is a groaning moan—it must be a ghost. Next a swishing witch sweeps by on her broomstick. And now there is a piercing, menacing shriek—the vampire is at work again.

Millions of children and adults cannot wait for this type of encounter. Wake any child the morning after Halloween, and the first words out of his or her mouth are sure to be, "What should I be next Halloween?" At Halloween, happiness and fun are often measured by how gruesome, ghastly, ghostly, scary, and horrifying a celebration you create. This is the time when gravestones are memorized and epitaphs echoed, when skeletons are funny and headless, bloody corpses are relished, when coffins are amusing and macabre monsters entertaining. The more imaginative, outrageous, and bizarre we are, the better.

For centuries Halloween has captured the hearts of children and adults. It was a different Halloween when the Celts occupied Europe, long before the birth of Christ. It was the time for all who lived good lives to feast, a kind of Thanksgiving. This All Hallow's Eve was also the night when ghosts and goblins walked the earth. People lit candles and masqueraded in frightening costumes made of animal skins to ward off the spirits of the dead, who returned to earth as wandering cats and witches and ghosts. The people in costumes began to visit homes, asking for treats—those who gave them would be assured of having a good year; those who did not were warned to watch out for evil spirits.

Thus this "Halloween," with its customs of offering thanksgiving for the harvest, wearing costumes to ward off evil spirits, and begging for food to ensure safe souls, soon spread. The Romans, after conquering England and France, introduced their own touches: they bobbed for apples and gave nuts to their neighbors. The Italians left bread and water, and lit lamps before going to bed to appease visiting ghosts. Other Europeans put out doughnuts and milk for the returning spirits, and still others placed empty chairs in a circle, one for each member of the family and one for an expected ghost.

In the nineteenth century, Irish immigrants brought the holiday to the United States, where it has evolved to become, in the last two decades, a national celebration.

Today's Halloween: A Family Holiday

Halloween has traditionally been a holiday for children. It was the children who dressed in imaginative costumes and paraded door to door, begging for treats. And it was the children who played mischievous tricks when they were not treated.

Today, Halloween has become our nation's Mardi Gras—a wonderful national family holiday. It is the perfect celebration for parents and children, enabling them to spend time together creating costumes, carving pumpkins, planning trick or treat activities, and participating in family parties. Halloween is the one time of the year when it is acceptable to act out many of our fantasies. On Halloween we can be scary or scared; we can look gruesome and ugly or ostentatiously beautiful. We can have fangs or smiles on our pumpkins and on our faces. We can be vampires or supermen or fairy princesses or belly dancers or bees or televisions—we can be anything!

For children, Halloween is an especially exciting time. It appeals to their imaginations, stimulating any inner urges to be something or someone else, to do things they would never think of doing on other days, to dress up as images they fantasize about or fear. At Halloween children can lose themselves in fun without having to worry about normal, proper, or appropriate behavior and dreams. They can be "grown up" by dressing up; they can go to parties and door to door at night; they can look silly or awful or glamorous, look any way they please; they can scare others and themselves; they can masquerade and fool those around them, calling attention to themselves. And, on Halloween, it's all right.

Dealing with Children's Fears

For some children, Halloween can be intimidating. According to child psychologist Dr. Lee Salk, such fears are normal, and Halloween is a good time for children to deal with them. Halloween allows anxieties and misgivings to come out into the open, letting children manage what is at other times nightmarish. It is a time that helps them deal with any fears of death, darkness, ghosts, and monsters openly, without the risk of being laughed at. Since Halloween is actually a publicly endorsed chance to be outrageous, it allows the child to become the "monster" of his or her fears.

It is important, at this time, to be extra sensitive to children's fears, however inexplicable or silly they may seem to adults. Dr. Salk explains, "Halloween today has a special significance because many children feel helpless in the face of violence on television, kidnappings, and other tragedies occurring in their world. So today the monsters under the bed that scare them are really the monsters inside their heads." And these monsters are different for every child. One child may be afraid of a ghost, but another may be afraid of clowns—and even though clowns may seem harmless to an adult, to a child they can be frightening and this fear must be understood. If your child shows some fears, urge him or her to express those fears and decide on a costume that he or she will love and not be frightened of wearing. For such a child, celebrate in a way that emphasizes the magical qualities of Halloween—the fantastic rather than the gruesome. Choose Cinderella or a magical harlequin rather than a tombstone or a witch. Remember that Halloween is just as much a holiday for fairy princesses as it is for ghouls.

Trick or Treat?

Some say it was the Celts who began the practice of trick or treating by offering to buy off evil people with treats before they turned on them with tricks. Others say it started with the Druids, Celtic priests who begged for favors in exchange for protection of souls, or with the Irish peasants, who begged for "soul cakes." It was the English who took it a step further—they put on masks and costumes as they begged for treats, and if their treats were not forthcoming, they played tricks.

The tradition has gone through many changes. Questions of the safety of treats and visiting unfamiliar homes have resulted in some parents discontinuing trick or treating, preferring instead to keep the celebrations at home. But in many communities trick or treating is still a favorite tradition. Here are some hints for a safer, happier Halloween:

• Have your child carry a flashlight, not only to help her see, but to help others see her.

• Watch out for dark costumes. If your child is dressed in black, add a white face if it is appropriate. Walking in lit areas with a flashlight will help prevent accidents.

Sarah Brokaw remembers trembling at the house where all trick or treaters encountered spooky music being played by a player piano. In order to get any candy, they had to lift a creaky old piano bench. It was scary!

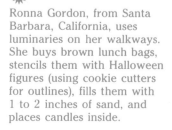

Ronna Gordon, from Santa Barbara, California, uses luminaries on her walkways. She buys brown lunch bags, stencils them with Halloween figures (using cookie cutters for outlines), fills them with 1 to 2 inches of sand, and places candles inside.

✳ Have a pre-Halloween party to get families together and prepare for Halloween. At this party you can carve pumpkins, make Plaster of Paris masks, put together trick or treat bags, and so on.

✳ Allen Beekman, a teacher in Albuquerque, New Mexico, was determined to give his trick or treaters healthy treats at his home. So he gave out figs and dates to each visiting child. The next morning, as he left for work, he found his front yard totally covered with the same figs and dates. Laments Mr. Beekman, "They didn't even make it to the sidewalk!"

• Trick or treat at homes your child knows.

• If you can, join your child. Children unaccompanied by an adult should always go in groups.

• Make sure your child wears a flame-resistant costume. Keep costumes short, or hold up long ones as he or she walks. Remind your child to keep an eye out at all times. He or she may find candles, forgotten tools, or broken or loose steps in other people's yards.

• Watch out for other people's pets. A thoughtless neighbor may leave his dogs out to roam. Be sure to shield your child from pets you do not know.

• The U.S. Consumer Product Safety Commission encourages parents to remind children *not to dart between cars*. Trick or treating is done at night when lighting in the streets can be poor. Drivers should be watching for trick or treaters but sometimes they do not. Try not to leave this to chance—prepare your children by reminding them to stay on the sidewalks and to cross the streets with an adult. If your neighborhood does not have sidewalks, do not trick or treat.

• The Consumer Product Safety Commission also warns children not to eat any candy before their parents check it out. It is unfortunate that this care must be taken, but it is a reality of life today. *Always* check for possible tampering with packages before letting children start on their treats.

• If a sword, cane, or stick is a part of your child's costume, make sure it is not sharp or too long. A child may be easily hurt by these accessories if he stumbles or trips.

• Try to dress the children in their own shoes. Wearing high heels or shoes that are too large can be dangerous and uncomfortable.

For those of you who expect and welcome trick or treaters, here are some thoughts:

• Have your treats prepared and by the door so you don't have to go looking for them. If you are handing out popcorn or cookies that you have made, have them prewrapped.

• Create a unique way to give out the treats. Simply placing the treats inside a carved-out pumpkin or in a basket makes them seem extra special.

• Clear your yard and walkways. Remove any obstacles (tools, ladders, skateboards, toys, stools) and repair any loose steps.

• Position pumpkins with candles in an area where they can still be seen but will not be in a child's way. Consider placing flashlights rather than candles in pumpkins that are outdoors.

• Replace lights or bulbs that are burnt out. A well-lit front yard and walkway is a safer one.

• Author Bud Trillin has said, ". . . giving trick or treaters raisins or apples or granola or wheat germ or mung-bean crackers is finklike behavior." We tend to agree. This is not the best time to make a point about nutrition.

The Penny Whistle Pumpkin Patch

Ever wonder how this pumpkin-carving tradition started? It is said it began with an Irishman named Jack, who was so evil and brazen that when he entered hell, he played tricks on the devil. The devil didn't take such behavior lightly, and banished Jack from hell, condemning him to walk the earth forever. Ever the scoundrel, Jack stole a hot piece of coal from hell and placed it inside a turnip that he had carved out. He held the turnip as a lantern and let it guide him as he wandered, looking for a final resting place. No one knows if Jack is still roaming the earth. But we do know that the jack-o'-lantern, now taking the form of a pumpkin, became the traditional light at Halloween.

You have probably carved a number of pumpkins, but if this year's inspiration for carving a pumpkin face is just like last year's and the year before that one, it is time to break out of the "pumpkin rut" and give your pumpkin a different personality. A pumpkin doesn't have to have that soulless, toothless grin. You've got choices to make!

The following are some general hints for pumpkin carving:

🟊 As an alternative to pumpkins, gourds make wonderful lanterns. They come in such unusual and natural shapes that when lit, they look splendid. The skin is tougher though, so you will need a drill to make random holes to create a face or interesting designs.

• Draw your face with markers before you begin to carve. This will save many mistakes!

• Place light sticks inside for a colored glow.

angle cut

• Always cut the top of the pumpkin off at an angle. If you cut it straight, the top will fall through in a day or so, when the heat of the candle distorts the shape and the pumpkin begins to shrivel up.

• Carve the pumpkin with a potato peeler, unserrated knife, ice-cream scoop, spoon, fork, and so forth.

• It is not necessary to cut the top off to put the candle inside. You can cut out a hole in the back and put the light in that way—this keeps the front and top of the pumpkin whole.

• Cut a notch out of the pumpkin's lid: this will allow the heat from the candle to escape and will prolong the life of the jack-o'-lantern.

NOTCH

• When you are finished carving your pumpkin, set a candle in melted wax on a jar lid and place it inside.

• Use mini flashlights inside the pumpkin—they are safer, and all you will need to replace are the batteries.

• The thinner the shell of your jack-o'-lantern (the more you have carved out), the brighter it will be—a thin shell allows more light to shine through.

• If you do not want to carve the pumpkin, use reflective tape cut in the shapes of eyes, nose, and mouth. The pumpkin will glow in the dark.

• A cluster of pumpkins is more effective than just one pumpkin. And duplicating the design of any one pumpkin is really effective: two or more screamers are better than one.

• If you have a walkway to your house, line the pumpkins on both sides and light with mini flashlights or candles.

✳ Joanna Seitz and daughter Amanda, from New Preston, Connecticut, cut their pumpkins in an unusual way. They slant the cut so the inside skin of the pumpkin is visible and then they paint each cutout with tempera, using a different color for each feature. When the candle inside is lit, the effect is colorfully spooky.

• Carve two different faces on opposite sides of the pumpkin. Carve a grin and a grimace for a theater mask.

• If you lose a piece of pumpkin while carving, just put it back in its place with toothpicks.

• To store pumpkins that you have not yet finished carving, or to keep carved pumpkins fresh in the daytime, wrap them loosely in plastic wrap and place in the refrigerator. Sealing them entirely or wrapping them too tightly will promote condensation and the growth of mold.

• Cookie cutters and other templates create repeated wraparound (all around the pumpkins) patterns. Put a cookie cutter up against the pumpkin and outline its shape with a felt-tip pen. Then cut it out with a sharp knife. Be sure to use cookie cutters that are not too detailed so the shape will not be too difficult to carve out. Hearts, rectangles, and other cookie cutters in familiar and funny shapes make terrific designs.

• Miniature pumpkins can be made into votive candleholders—cut off the top, scoop out the pulp and seeds, and light. They can also be used for serving desserts (see page 68).

• Make a pyramid of pumpkins. Carve five or six pumpkins and join them together horizontally with dowels to form a base. Form another, shorter row (three or four pumpkins) on top of that and yet another, even shorter row (one or two pumpkins) on top of the second. The result is a pyramid of pumpkins that can be used as a centerpiece or at the entrance to the house. Light them with candles.

• Carve out just the eyes for a ghostlike look.

• Carve facial features at an angle (see our illustration of a howling pumpkin) instead of straight on—it gives the pumpkin a spooky look.

• Pumpkins also make great vases—hollow out and fill with water and flowers, or skip the water and use dried flowers and branches of leaves.

PENNY WHISTLE PUMPKINS:

▲ An unusual two-faced pumpkin: make a smile on one side and a frown on the other, or a vampire on one side (cut out sharp, fang-like teeth) and a vamp on the other (cut out a wide-lip mouth or paint red lips).

• Paint a face directly on the pumpkin.

▲ Cluster several small faces together on one pumpkin. It is more effective if you can place them at different heights and close together.

▲ Repeat a design on the same pumpkin. Try carving a pumpkin with hearts or clovers cut out all over it.

► Pumpkin house: make windows, a door, and a path of candy leading up to the door. You can even make curtains out of handkerchiefs.

▲ Turn a pumpkin into Cinderella's Coach. Use slices of butternut squash for wheels, a gowned miniature doll inside the carved-out window, plastic horses with ribbon reins, and more ribbons and silk flowers for decoration.

► Make line drawings with knives (you do not cut all the way through). Cut thin slivers, about ¼ inch wide and spaced about ½ inch apart so the slices will not fall apart (what you are doing is slicing through rather than cutting pieces out). Use a sharp paring knife.

◄ Make a pumpkin vegetable patch. Do not carve out the pumpkin. Get a large pumpkin and stick on various vegetables with toothpicks to create a face: curly lettuce makes great hair—use lots of it; zucchini slices pinned flat for the eyes (with raisins as pupils); a green bean for the mouth (or use white beans for the teeth—glue them across the front); a beet for the nose (or a chili pepper with the curve going down); and baby squash for ears.

➤Diorama: carve out the front with a jagged edge instead of removing the top. This can become a setting for a scene you want to create. Place different miniature Halloween toys, dolls, animals, and so forth inside. Insert a flashlight into a small hole in the back for lighting.

▲Pumpkin scarecrow: stack graduated sizes of pumpkins one on top of the other, starting with a very large one on the bottom. Carve only the top one in an unusual face. Use smaller pumpkins, attached with stakes, for arms. Lean the scarecrow against the house and surround with corn stalks.

◀Pumpkin centerpiece: hollow out the pumpkin, line with foil or plastic wrap, and fill with miniature wrapped gifts, each tied with a ribbon. The ribbons should cascade out of the pumpkin and onto the table.

➤Place the decorated pumpkin on top of two shoes: slippers and men's shoes work well because the pumpkin will sit on the openings and the fronts of the shoes will stick out.

▲ Gather a family of pumpkins: father, mother, and kids (use the miniature pumpkins for kids). Perch eyeglasses on a protruding carrot nose for the dad; the mom has a hat with a veil and earrings; the baby has a diaper and pins, and a bottle or pacifier sticking out of its round mouth.

◀Pumpkin man or woman: put together a pumpkin person with a pumpkin head and old pants and a shirt stuffed with newspapers or other old rags for a body. Fasten the shirt tail to the pants (or stuff into the pants) and set the "person" in a large chair or out on the porch. Paint a face on the pumpkin. Top with a hat, throw a scarf around the neck, place a pipe in the mouth, and you have a pumpkin person. Women's clothing, complete with high heels, jewelry, and hat, also works well.

MAKE A CHARACTER PUMPKIN:

Hobo: place straw on the head or hanging out of the mouth.

Fancy lady: glue fake eyelashes and draw longer ones with a felt-tip pen; make an exaggerated mouth with painted red lips; stick cheap rhinestone earrings into the sides as ears.

Magician: put a top hat with a stuffed bunny in it upside down on the head. Surround with playing cards and a wand.

Baseball player: place baseballs in the cut-out eyes, your favorite team's hat on top, a small bat alongside, and baseball cards stuck into the sides as ears (make a slit in the side of the pumpkin and slide the cards into it).

Fortuneteller: wrap a scarf around the head and tie it to one side; place cards alongside and a crystal ball in front.

MAKE A FAMOUS FACE PUMPKIN:

Charlie Chaplin: paint on a mustache and top with a bowler.

The Lone Ranger: paint a mask on or use a black eye mask.

Roger Rabbit or Bugs Bunny: top with a headband with rabbit ears and stick a carrot with greens in a carved-out mouth with one tooth.

Groucho Marx: paint on a mustache and stick a cigar in the carved-out mouth.

It's All About Costumes

Becoming someone else is a fantasy come true. Halloween allows children of all ages to be whatever they want, and, on just this one day, the crazier the costume, the better. Once the commitment to dress up has been made, it is almost impossible not to have fun.

Disguises allow everyone to be an actor. Costumes transform far more than outward appearances; they allow people to forget themselves and to be whatever they can imagine and create.

Unless it is a toddler you are dressing up, choosing the costume for your child can be a dangerous proposition. Self-determination is the name of the game. Parental input in the way of theme suggestions and in the execution are usually all that is needed. It is really your child's choice. The words you do not want to hear the day after Halloween are a wistful, "But I really wanted to be . . . !" Sarah Brokaw, now nineteen, is still trying to live down the Halloween when her mother dressed her up like a pumpkin. It was not that another choice had been turned down; rather, on that day, Sarah would have preferred to be *anything* but a pumpkin.

If there is anything that should be called the official Halloween fabric, it is felt. It comes in vibrant colors and you don't need to sew it—you just glue it together. You can punch holes in it and lace it up. And all those wonderful sparkly trimmings—glitter, lace, sequins, lamé, fake fur—all glue easily to felt.

Molly Damm, age nine, has been keeping a costume drawer her whole life. All her friends and relatives save their collectibles, especially old costume jewelry, and give them to Molly, who loves to dress up all year round. Come Halloween, the best costumes are made from the treasures in her drawer. But, best of all for Molly, if she wants to dress up on any day, her mother allows it, within reason, believing it allows Molly to learn how to express herself.

A similar thing, sort of, happened to Lindsay Feldman when she was three. Mom Trisha could not resist and bought Lindsay the most beautiful bee costume, perfect in every detail. But Lindsay wanted to be a fairy godmother. Besides, she told her mom, she hated bees and she hated yellow and she hated stripes. So Trisha, who collects clothes all year long for Lindsay to use for dressing up, decided to concoct a fairy godmother costume out of old petticoats and lace that were in her closet, even making a rhinestone tiara for Lindsay. It was quite a shock, then, to return home from trick or treating only to hear Lindsay say to her grandmother on the phone, "Mommy made me a pretty costume, Grandma. But there was a really, really pretty bee in front of me when we went trick or treating and she buzzed and buzzed so loud that they gave her all the candy!"

Halloween is a chance for children to use their own imaginations with fewer restrictions than they face in everyday life. There are no penalties or rewards based on the decision to be a witch instead of a gypsy! Simply creating a costume is its own payoff. It does not have to be elaborate, sophisticated, or expensive. It just has to be your own. With a few handy tools—staple gun, glue gun, Elmer's glue, clear packing tape, needle and thread, and plenty of enthusiasm—you and your child can achieve some remarkable transformations.

Ghosts, goblins, witches, vampires, clowns, ballerinas, pirates, princesses, and gypsies appear every Halloween. These old standards in the world of costumes are popular year after year for a reason: they are simple; they are immediately recognizable; they are symbols of Halloween; and they work. Every year has its fads: one year will produce as many punk rockers as the next will see Ninjas. But old favorites still dominate.

While it is easy to assume that a ghost is just a ghost, it does not seem to work out that way. Even the most common costumes can be individualized. Marc Gilbar's ghost had no twin. He had a lopsided grin, wore green "glop" splattered across the front (he was an intentionally sloppy ghost), and carried a backpack with a hidden tape recorder that played the theme from *Ghostbusters*.

Lisa Gilbar's last witch was a glamorous trollop. From the rhinestone necklaces hanging from a red satin cape to the glittery black hat with feathers at the top, this was one unique witch. Another little friend combined a red yarn Raggedy Ann wig with her witch's outfit for a completely different effect. And our friend Andrea Hirshhorn was once a gray cat, a kind of bag-lady cat, with torn, mismatched sneakers, wrinkles between her whiskers, and a monocle in one eye, carrying a shopping bag full of newspapers and rags.

The variations on the same theme are endless. However, if this year there is a search going on at your house for some new ideas or ways of embellishing the old ones, there may be inspiration in the list on the following pages. These costume ideas require only a few props, some makeup, and a touch of your own invention and imagination.

THE PENNY WHISTLE COSTUME CLOSET:

Spider = black leotard and tights + three pairs of black panty hose stuffed with old nylons (stitch the hose to the waist of the leotard) + stocking cap + pipe cleaners painted black as antennae

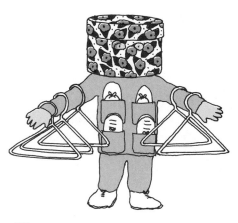

Closet = wire hangers hanging from clothes + hat box on head + shoe bags pinned on clothes

Robot = cardboard box with holes for arms and legs + box for head + headlights on chest + light sticks for antennae + silver paint

Jack-in-the-box = cardboard box + Slinky toys for arms + stocking cap

Television = cardboard box +gelatin paper covering hole + flashlight held inside + light stick antennae

Gift = cardboard box + wrapping paper + ribbons on head and shoes

Dice = boxes for body + painted dots + polka dot headdress

Pippi Longstocking = hair sprayed red + pipe cleaners in braids + mismatched clothes + black freckles on face

Mummy = jelled hair pulled away from face + white makeup on face + strips of muslin wrapped around entire body

Skeleton = black leotard and tights + white tape or chalk for ribs and bones + white makeup on face with black eyes

Traffic light = black leotard and tights + three large satin circles (red, green, and yellow) sewed on front

Ice-cream soda = cardboard cut in the shape of a soda glass + fiberfill sprayed pink + cardboard tube wrapped in striped paper for a straw

Comic fairy godmother = wings + white wig + magic wand + silly makeup + mismatched clothes + hula hoop taped under full skirt

Swimming pool = blue leotard and tights and blue wig + headband with cardboard diving board attached + mini doll on board

Mermaid = flesh-colored leotard + bikini + gelatin paper wrapped around lower body + cut-out fin strapped on belt + flippers + long yellow wig

Kitchen = hanging pots and pans + measuring spoons and sponges + colander hat

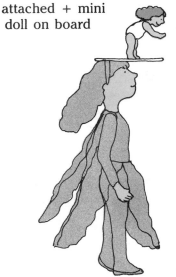

Garbage can = rubber wastebasket minus bottom with cut-out arm holes + top lid hat + glued-on colorful identifiable garbage (empty boxes or cans, crumpled aluminum foil) + a stuffed raccoon hanging onto the side

Graffiti pad = white sweatsuit + hanging markers (other revelers get to write messages)

Crayon = one-color bodysuit + felt cone hat made of the same color

Carrot = orange bodysuit + green mousse in hair + green face paint

Tossed green salad = glued green leaves on mask, hat, and green leotard + bell pepper belt + carrot necklace + empty plastic salad-dressing bottle on hat

Three blind mice = three people in tuxedos + dark sunglasses + canes + felt mice ears

Money tree = green sweatsuit + fake money glued on the suit

Hot-air balloon = large straw basket with holes for legs + ribbons + large helium balloons attached to the basket

Queen of hearts = heart cards glued on white outfit + top hat with hearts + red hearts on cheeks

Fisherman = yellow rain slicker + fishing pole + net or bait bucket (useful trick or treat container)

Tourist = colorful wild shirt + shorts + several cameras around neck + sunglasses + hat

Disk jockey = hip outfit + records hanging from clothes + sunglasses + walkman

Skin diver = wet suit + goggles + flippers + bucket with plastic fish

Grapes = green or purple leotard and tights + balloons safety-pinned to clothes + stretch headband

Statue of Liberty = green sheet draped over body + green crown + torch with flashlight + book

Prisoner = striped clothes + striped cap + ball and chain on legs + white makeup on face and black under eyes

Floor lamp = one-color bodysuit + lamp shade for hat + bulb with battery or flashlight

Thermometer = silver bicycle helmet + straight white shift + scale with red "mercury" line drawn with felt-tip marker

GROUP COSTUMES

CAT AND MOUSE

ANY TWINS

THE SUPREMES OR SINGER WITH BACKUPS

A GROUP OF PENGUINS (TUXEDOS AND NOSES)

A BOX OF CRAYONS

MOTHER HEN AND HER FLOCK

SNOW WHITE AND YOUR VERSION OF HER DWARFS

✳
Peter Gordon, who owns
Bambi Toys, reminds all his
customers that comfort is a
big key to having fun. When
designing your own costume,
think about what you will be
doing all evening. Be com-
fortable. Children will probably not be relaxed or safe in
high heels. Costumes that are
taped together and are fragile
will also cause tears if they
come apart.

TRICKS
OF THE
TRADE

cleansing cream
water
tissues
cotton swabs
brushes
washcloths
glue
scissors
vaseline
cold cream
and/or shampoo

spirit gum

spirit gum
remover or
acetone

A Word About Costumes and Makeup

No matter how carefully you have chosen your costume, no matter how elaborate or accurate it is, without makeup it is unfinished. Makeup is the perfect way to complete the illusion. It allows you to emerge as a new crea-tion. It makes you authentic: you can't be an old man without wrinkles on your face; you can't be a ghost without a white face; and you can't be a pirate without a stubble beard.

There are some tricks of the trade you can adapt. Try not to rule out simple transformations. Even a white face or a line or two drawn with an eyebrow pencil can achieve a desired effect. Master craftsmen like Dick Smith add decades to a man's life by simply placing a few strategic wrinkles. Smith whitewashes a face and adds dark shadows, and a mild-mannered young man turns into a hair-raising werewolf. He glues scars and warts onto a face and adds protruding eyeballs, and a monster emerges.

There are many makeup kits on the market containing makeup and accessories (noses, scars, fangs, and so forth) that will remake your face into an unforgettable creation. But remember—most people using makeup for Hallo-ween do not use it any other time of the year, and they need to ask some questions: Does it wear well? Does it come off easily? Does it leave the skin in good condition? Is it user-safe? Will it cause any allergic reaction?

TRICKS OF THE TRADE

Here are some pointers from Imagineering (a company that manufactures FDS-approved costume makeup) to be aware of when buying costume makeup.

• Don't worry about scent. Most "novelty" makeup, sold for use at Hallo-ween, is unscented.
• Color pigment is a common culprit of skin irritation. All manufacturers use the same color pigments, so if you get a reaction to one, you will get the same reaction to others.
• Read the list of ingredients: the *simplest formulations,* with the fewest ingredients, cause the least amount of irritation. And look for FDA approval on any makeup package. The FDA uses the Cosmetology Institute guidelines on makeup before approving a makeup product.
• You will find the words "hypo-allergenic," "laboratory tested," "safe," or "nontoxic" on some packaging. These are makeups that the manufacturer has already tested.
• Cream makeup is better than greasepaint because it is less greasy. It is easy to apply and to remove with cold cream. Use it instead of pancake makeup, which can irritate.

THE BASICS

- Always begin any makeup application with a clean face. When dye is combined with dirt it is harder to remove.
- Splash the face with cold water to close the skin pores. This will help prevent makeup from absorbing into the skin.
- Put a thin layer of cold cream or Vaseline on the face before applying makeup.
- Whatever makeup look you create, exaggerate! This is no time for subtleties. If you make eyelashes, draw them thick and high. If you rouge your face, make it red, not pink. If you are using white makeup for your face, make it cover the whole face. If you are creating expressions, reshape your eyebrows into a high arch and redraw your mouth for a true scowl.
- Work from a picture—whether it is an animal or a fairy godmother, work out the details on paper first.
- In most face-makeup designs, it is the eyes that are most important. The eyes will hold the spotlight, but they are also sensitive and fragile. Be sure to keep all makeup away from the eyes themselves. You can paint the lids, shadow under the eyes, and draw wrinkles around the eyes, without getting anything *in* the eyes.
- Actors have long used Johnson's Baby Shampoo to remove makeup and glue. It dissolves theater makeup easily, gently, and painlessly.
- It is always best to test the makeup on your body the night before, just in case you may be allergic to it. Spread a little on your forearm. The same goes for acetone used to remove makeup.

Make up your face in two halves—one half is pretty and normal, the other half is a monster.

SOME SPECIAL TRICKS

- For any Halloween spirit, ghost, witch, ghoul, or monster, start with white foundation all over the face and black makeup under and over the eyes. This will be your "canvas." You can then individualize your creation by adding wrinkles, colored scars or bloody wounds, skeleton teeth, and so on.
- For a "beautiful" face—princess, queen, movie star, bride, or doll—apply a flesh-colored foundation all over the face and then add the same touches that Mom would add to her "glamorous" face (eyeshadow, eyelashes, rouge, red lipstick), but really make them stand out. If you cannot see the makeup from across the room, apply more.
- Mom's eyebrow pencil will produce amazing effects all by itself. Join eyebrows to make one continuous brow, make stubble for a beard, or draw a pencil mustache and lines for wrinkles.
- Draw and outline teeth on the upper and lower lips for a superb skeleton.
- Hollywood makeup artist Patricia Messina makes imaginative use of Streaks and Tips hair spray. She suggests experimenting with your own hair color or turning an old wig into a striped fantasy. She has also streaked animal headpieces, giving them a truly original look. Streaks and Tips comes in crazy colors, and instantly and easily transforms your whole head. It washes out with shampoo.

Larry Liff, today the president of Imagineering (a makeup manufacturer), used to work as a makeup artist at Burbank Studios. When he was a kid, he couldn't wait for Halloween because tricking was his passion. One year, at school, he put a sponge dipped in red sugar water under his tongue. Then he stood in front of his class, hit himself in the stomach, and spurted out the "blood." Naturally, he was a big hit!

❋ Dr. Dean Donaldson, a dentist in Sun Valley, Idaho, dresses up as a tooth every year at Halloween. He also gives out toothbrushes to trick or treaters.

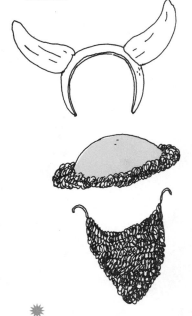

❋ For little kids, you can do great things with Dad's Bermuda shorts and suspenders. They are the right length and are baggy so little kids can easily become hobos and clowns. Beau Pittman was a hobo: Dad's Bermuda shorts + suspenders + blue wig + striped shirt + red nose.

• The Ben Nye Company, founded by the late Hollywood makeup artist and now run by his son Dana, makes Wrinkle Stipple. This is a way of aging your face. The instructions on the package are simple to follow. Basically you scrunch up the face and put on the stipple in thin layers with a dry sponge. The result is an old face formed by accentuating your own wrinkles. It is easy to remove and is available at some beauty-supply stores all year round and at Halloween centers in the fall.

Other makeup kits abound at Halloween. Imagineering makes some popular kits that are complete with everything you will need. Woochie Company makes inexpensive clown and werewolf noses, bald caps, slit throats, warts, bullet holes, devil horns, witch noses, and gross cuts.

• Patricia Messina uses "crepe wool," imitation hair made of wool, that comes braided in all colors and is held together with a string. You cut the string, wet the hair, and then form it into whatever shape you like by stretching it, wrapping it around a chair, or hanging it to dry. The more you stretch it, the less curly it gets. On your head it will create any hairdo. On the face you can make your own unique beard or mustache—you just pull the hair apart, cut it, and glue. It is great for creating old men, werewolves, pirates, and the like, and is found in large beauty-supply stores.

• Press-on fingernails make an instant impact. They come in many lengths and colors and are easy to put on and remove. Witches and vampires as well as queens and other glamorous women love long nails.

• Spirit gum will glue hair and plastic scars onto the face. It is easy to remove with alcohol, acetone, or other removal lotions.

• There is an old theater trick used by actors to create a "5 o'clock shadow." You can create a stubbled beard by pressing a stipple sponge into dark brown makeup and dabbing it on your face. The sponge is black with holes and is available at beauty-supply stores. It will not smudge and is particularly good for younger kids who may not like wearing masks or beards.

• White water-based shoe polish added to your hair creates a great effect. It comes out with shampoo.

• Make eyebrows disappear by making a thick paste with soap and water and pressing onto your brows. (Ivory Soap works great—don't use a deodorant soap, which is not good for your face.) Let dry, then do it again. After the second application dries, cover with foundation. Eyebrows will have disappeared and you can draw new shapes in their place or remain eyebrowless. Great for clowns, witches, vampires, and so on.

• Glycerine will give the illusion of sweating. A few drops placed on the face with a sponge will stay there for a quite a while.

• For younger children, you can rely on "makeup props" that do not need to be applied to the face. Hats, wigs, glasses, jewelry, and scarves all create effective illusions without a lot of fuss.

Halloween Parties

There is no better way to celebrate Halloween than with a family party. Other than birthday parties, Halloween parties are the ones children enjoy best and remember forever. Planning the party together is a wonderful opportunity to spend time with your children. The following Penny Whistle Party Planning Principles will send you on your way.

PENNY WHISTLE PRINCIPLES

1. When we say "you," we mean you and your child. Involve your child at every stage of planning. Participation is critical to making your child feel important.

2. If this is your child's first Halloween, make it lighthearted and pleasant. Emphasize "happy" pumpkins rather than scowling ones; make witches silly rather than scary; make costumes whimsical or beautiful rather than intimidating or menacing. Tone down the terror and go for the fantasy— at least the first time around.

3. Plan ahead! Give yourself plenty of time to plan your Halloween party. Try to start four weeks ahead of time. Finding decorations, music tapes, and items needed for games and activities all take legwork and time. Give yourself a leisurely pace rather than doing it all in a frantic frenzy.

4. Personal touches will make your party unforgettable. Even though it may take longer to plan and make things yourself, in our experience, children and adults alike always appreciate the special care that results in an exceptional party.

5. Plan activities for every moment of the party. A party is like theater: you have a beginning, a middle, and an end. Having a complete plan will give you a feeling of great control, will minimize potential problems, and will virtually guarantee that your party will be a smash.

6. Take part in the party. Don't stay in the kitchen or watch from the sidelines. Participate in the activities as much as you can.

7. Get help! No one expects you to do it all alone—and you shouldn't expect it of yourself. Ask neighbors and family to chip in. Get some students to help with the children. And if you are short of time or temper, buy something that is ready-made instead of making it yourself. We all need help—remember to ask for it.

8. As you read through the parties, note the suggested ages for each. Some parties are more appropriate for older kids than others, and vice versa. Our guidelines are general and should suit most kids. But be flexible. If the children are mature enough to handle a scarier party than the one we have suggested for their age, choose activities that are more suitable for them.

9. Speaking of flexibility, these parties are structured so that any activity, decoration, or food can be easily transferred from one party to another. If you find a game your child is anxious to play but it's not in the party you chose, move it and adapt it to your needs. You can do that with everything in this book. Remember, our suggestions are just that—it is your added imagination, creativity, and requirements that will make your party uniquely yours. You will also find that there are probably more game suggestions for a party than you will need. We believe being prepared with more than you need is better than being caught with extra time on your hands. Just remember that you do not have to play every game.

10. Take photographs! Both you and your children will want to remember your party. All too often the taking of pictures gets lost in the excitement of the party. Assign this task to one of your helpers. If you have a video camera, take movies and then play them back before the children leave. Seeing themselves in their costumes will make their day! Polaroid snapshots of the children in their creations make wonderful party favors. If you are using 35mm film, you may want to duplicate special photographs of the guests and send them after the party.

11. Invitations set the stage and mood for the party. Make them inventive and, if at all possible, send them at least three weeks ahead of time. Each party idea has a suggested invitation or two. Some have drawings you can photocopy. Do not hesitate to add your own personal touch to these invitations, or choose an invitation from one party and adapt it to another.

12. Creating an entertaining atmosphere is particularly important. In the *Penny Whistle Party Planner*, we suggested that, when it comes to decorating parties, less is more—overdecorating is unnecessary and may, in fact, overwhelm your child. But Halloween is different. You really cannot have too many cobwebs, ghosts, witches, tombstones, or skeletons. Go to it—the works will work!

13. At the end of each party, you will find a suggested menu. The recipes can be found at the end of the book. If you want to switch dishes from one party to another, do it. If you are overwhelmed with plans and would rather order a pizza, do it!

14. Be prepared for the unexpected:
- Have extra food and drinks, favors, props, and light bulbs.
- Have a fire extinguisher in working order and in the house, especially if you are using candles for decoration.
- Have a complete medical kit at hand.

BARNYARD BASH

AGES 2–5

Instead of those ghosts and goblins for fright,
We picked something else for this Halloween night,
We thought and we thought and it came in a flash,
Why not dress up as animals for a Barnyard Bash!

Instead of those witches and monsters and fools,
Those scary old skeletons, those haunted old ghouls,
We invite you to come as a kitten or dove,
A puppy, a tiger—any animal you love!

We're having an old-fashioned barnyard affair,
Where scarecrows and pigs and roosters can share
A fabulous party, with races and games,
It's a special Halloween, so send over your names.

We'll see you on Halloween night, do arrive
Dressed as a barnyard native, come around five,
879 Elm Street, come by car or by jet,
We promise a Halloween you'll never forget!

INVITATION

Have your child choose a cookie cutter in the shape of an animal he or she loves or make a template out of cardboard to use as a pattern on colored stock. You can use different animals on different colored papers. Cut out the individual invitations. Type or write the poem on page 28 and photocopy. Glue the poem onto each animal invitation. Be sure to sign the invitation and include your phone number so guests can RSVP.

As an alternative to using the poem, buy dog bones made out of rawhide and available at the market or pet store. Use a felt-tip pen to write out simple invitation copy. Mail in a padded envelope.

We'll see you on Halloween night do arrive
Dressed as a barnyard native, come around five,
879 Elm Street, come by car or by jet
We promise a Halloween you'll never forget.

You are invi

Lynda Guber, from Los Angeles, gives a Halloween party every year—after all, it is also her birthday. Her favorite trick: she cuts hundreds of gold and silver stars in all sizes out of shiny paper and hangs them from the ceiling with strings.

DECORATIONS

1. If it is warm where you live, you have a distinct advantage: creating a farm outdoors is a natural. But you can easily turn your party room into a farm. If available, a bale or two of hay and several bunches of dried cornstalks will set the stage nicely. If not, autumn leaves, pumpkins, gourds, and cobs of dried corn will work perfectly. A collection of your indoor plants will add to the barnyard feel. Buy western bandannas and either collect wood sticks or buy wood dowels in about 18-inch lengths. The food will be served in the bandannas, which get attached to the sticks. Place them together against a wall.
2. Make a scarecrow or two out of old clothes, such as jeans, a plaid shirt, and worn-out sneakers or boots. Stuff the figure with straw and rags, and place him in a sitting position on a chair. Add a head made out of a pumpkin, with a face carved out, and top with an old cowboy hat.
3. Place pumpkins everywhere, some carved and others not. Insert flashlights instead of candles inside the pumpkins so you will not have to worry about potential accidents.
4. If finding a parrot to borrow or rent for the party is not too difficult an assignment, do it! They make big impressions on little people.

Halloween lends itself to all kinds of contests. Have one for the best carved pumpkin, or the wittiest, strangest, scariest, or most colorful costumes and pumpkins.

29

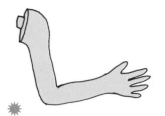

* Rob and Bobbi Gordon of Detroit, Michigan, create an unforgettable set outside their home. One of their favorite gimmicks is to use mannequins placed all over the front yard. They buy several and dismantle their parts— thus some are armless and others have only one leg. There is always one who is headless, holding her head in her arms. Some have red paint on them as if blood was splattered on them.

* Get a witch, ghost, or pumpkin piñata and fill it with trick or treat candy. It provides both an activity and a decoration.

ACTIVITIES

1. Trick or Treat Bags—It is always useful to have an activity in progress to accommodate different arrival times. Decorating brown paper shopping bags, collected from your grocery store, as trick or treat bags should appeal to all children. Provide felt-tip markers, Halloween stickers, cut-out pumpkins, cutouts of ghosts and bats, and some small candies and lollipops as favors to add to the bags at the end of the party.

2. Barnyard Mural—Mural painting is especially designed for outdoor fun, but if you are lucky enough to have a wall in a casual place, like the inside wall of your garage or basement, you can paper a wall and turn the artists loose. Use 2 or 3 yards of butcher paper. Tape it to the wall with masking tape. Place wide-tipped markers in all colors in plastic cups. The children can draw on the paper or paste on cutouts of Halloween and animal shapes. You may be surprised by the creativity. It does not matter if the children are the only ones who see a barnyard in their work. Use the scene as a backdrop for photographs you may wish to take of the menagerie.

3. Feed the Pony—Divide the guests into two teams. Give each team a soup spoon filled with popcorn. Have them form two lines at one end of the room. The object is to carry the soup spoon of popcorn to the other side of the room and back, "feeding the pony" by passing it on to the next team member, until the last person has carried the popcorn across the room and back. If any of the kernels fall off, the carrier must stop to pick them up. The team finishing first wins.

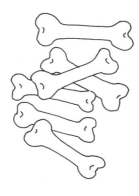

4. The Groaning Ghost—Compose a simple and goofy story about a ghost, using words that match with sounds. As you tell the story to the children, whenever a certain word is mentioned, the children make that sound. For example: a ghost brings a groan; a witch, a cackle; a goblin, a hiss; a cat, a meow; a bat, a squeak; a monster, a shriek; a vampire, a sucking sound; and so on. If you want to stick strictly to the barnyard theme, you can play this game with animal sounds instead.

5. Vanished Barnyard Bones—The farmer's dog has been hiding bones for years. They are hidden all over the farm. Cut small bones out of cardboard, or you may wish to buy plastic skeleton bones. Hide them around the room. The child who finds the most bones wins. Playing some music will make the scramble for bones more fun.

6. Fill the Farm—Someone has stolen all the animals on the farm, and the farm is now empty. The children must find the animals. Buy a bag of small rubber animals—many packages come with farm and jungle animals. Hide them all over the party room. When it is time to play this game, give each child a small bag and have them find the animals. The first one to find a certain number of animals wins, or the first to find three little pigs, or the first to find a blue dinosaur, and so on.

What's a ghost's favorite ride?
A roller ghoster.

Around Halloween one year, teacher Iris Brooks held a Charlotte's Web party, inviting all the children to come as the different characters in the book. The kids loved seeing the various individualized versions of Charlotte, Templeton the rat, Mr. Zuckerman, and, of course, Wilbur the pig. Iris has given this costume party with other books and has found that kids always love to come as characters from the books they read.

7. Tagging the Donkey's Tail—You need a large space for this game, and a couple of adult helpers to make sure the running kids do not get out of control. Divide the players into two teams in two rows, one child standing behind the other, each with his hands on the shoulders of the person in front of him. The first child in each row is the "donkey," and the last child is the "tail." The object is to have each donkey tag the other's tail. Obviously, both donkeys must try to keep their tails from being tagged—the rows turn and meander all over the room. When one donkey tags the other donkey's tail, he becomes the tail and the next person in line becomes the new donkey.

31

PRIZES

Favors and prizes can be those little rubber animals that are part of the farm game, and the decorated trick or treat bags with the candies you put in them at the end. A paperback copy of *Charlotte's Web* by E. B. White is always a special treat.

Wear garlic at Halloween— it keeps the vampires away.

S·N·A·C·K·S

Pumpkin Bread
Sugar Cookie Pumpkins
Worms
Raisins
Gummy Snakes
Juice

Make pumpkin balls by wrapping trick or treat candies or toys in strips of orange crepe paper. Keep wrapping round and round until you see the shape of a pumpkin. Draw eyes and mouth with a black felt-tip pen.

This is a picnic, so the food is wrapped as in a picnic and placed in bandannas that are tied to sticks or wooden dowels.

WITCHES, WIZARDS, AND GOBLINS GANG

AGES 2-5

It's the Witches, Wizards, and Goblins Gang, and they are out to make Halloween a hoot. For younger children, it is important to take the fear out of Halloween, to make their early experiences a combination of acceptable scary feelings and a lot of fun. This party works both as an introduction to Halloween for those impressionable two-year-olds and as a stimulating celebration for the more sophisticated five-year-olds.

If the salt shaker falls, quickly throw some salt over your left shoulder to bring back good luck.

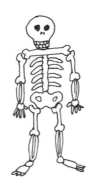

Artist Richard Mann, from Santa Barbara, California, would rather be the tricker than the treater. He creates a haunted house in his garage full of inflatable spiders and skeletons hanging on netting he buys at the local plant nursery. He places an inflatable spider on the netting so it looks like it's just hanging on, and uses a dimmer switch so he can turn the lights up or down according to the ages of the children who come to trick or treat. Richard has also been known to dress up in a gorilla suit to surprise his visitors.

INVITATION

Buy black magic wands. Dress them up with orange and black satin ribbons. Attach the following invitation to each wand with the ribbons.

Bring this wand to Enter the MAGICAL WORLD of the WITCHES, WIZARDS, & GOBLINS GANG
DRESS: your own creation
Gang meets on October 31 at 6:00pm, 555 Belwood Drive
PLEASE SAY A MAGICAL YES: 555-6789

DECORATIONS

1. This party is a combination of wizardry and ghosts. Start by making a supernatural entrance for your guests. Place the host or another person at the front door with a tape recorder. Whenever the doorbell rings, he or she will press the "play" button and a funny message previously taped by your child will be heard: "Welcome, come in, if you dare. Walk on in and hold your hair!" or "Hocus-pocus, wizards and kings, enter dancing while you sing!"

2. String tiny Christmas tree lights around the door frame leading to the party room.

3. Hang lots of silver and gold stars with clear fishing line from the ceiling. Buy them at a party supply store or make them yourself—the more, the prettier. You can also tent the room. This requires attaching a cloth to the ceiling in the center of the room and in each corner (use pins or a staple gun). Parachutes from army/navy surplus stores work perfectly. You can also use king-size sheets.

4. Balloons are always festive. Mylar ones are great and will last longer than latex when filled with helium, but they are more expensive. Black rubber latex balloons are especially effective for Halloween, or try combining a variety of colors.

5. Cut out ghosts and witches from Mylar paper and hang them from the ceiling.

6. Glow-in-the-dark tape is especially pretty when the lights are low. Put it on lamps, tables, walls, balloons, and so on. Don't worry, you can peel it right off.

7. Make ghost necklaces a couple of days before the party to hang as decorations and then to give away as party favors. Drip a glob of Elmer's glue, the size of a half dollar, on wax paper. Make sure the glob is uneven so it will look like a ghost. Let it dry for two days. When dried, draw eyes on each glob with a black felt-tip marker. Punch a hole at the top of each glob and pull black yarn through it.

34

ACTIVITIES

1. Scaredy Cats—With your instant Polaroid camera, have each child lie on a bed with his or her hair spread up and out. Take the picture. When it is ready, turn it upside down and presto, you have a photo of a child with his or her hair standing on end, looking "scared to death." Of course, facial expressions count a lot here. Short-haired kids can get in on the act if you provide a wig as a photographer's prop.

2. Pumpkin Paradise—Young children, and even some adults, have trouble carving pumpkins. How about painting and/or decorating them? Some of the pumpkins you plan to paint should be partially carved out ahead of time so the children can paint around the cutouts and inside the edges. For decorating pumpkins, get assorted vegetables and toothpicks. There are some very bizarre faces that can be made with other foods.

3. War of the Witches—Have the children stand in a circle holding hands. One child, who plays the wicked witch, stands outside the circle. Another child, who plays the witch's dinner, stands inside the circle. Both players can fly in and out of the circle whenever they want to, but the children in the circle will help the victim by raising and lowering their arms to keep the witch from getting her dinner. The rules are: no bending of knees and no kicking the witch. When the witch does catch the victim, they both join the circle and the players to the right of each child take their places for the next round. If you have a lot of kids you can have two witches and two victims.

4. Black Cat and Her Kittens—Have the children choose a child to be the black cat. The black cat must leave the room. Seated around a table, the children place their arms on the table with heads on their arms, so they cannot see what is going on in the room. The person in charge of the game will tap several of the children and explain to them that those tapped children will become the "kittens," who will meow at the black cat. The black cat is then called into the room and the kittens will begin to meow for their mother. The black cat has to identify her kittens. The first kitten to be identified becomes the black cat in the next round. The cat has to continue searching until she has found all her kittens.

HERE LIES GOOD OLD BILL
HE ALWAYS LIED
AND ALWAYS WILL
HE ONCE LIED OUT LOUD
AND NOW HE LIES STILL.

Want to have the spookiest spiders ever? Keita Metz, from Lyme, New Hampshire, buys crab shells at the local market, the extra ones they use for display. She spray paints them black and, on Halloween night, puts them around the table and hangs them from fishing wire.

5. Magic Show—Ask an amateur magician from your local high school or community to perform. Request that he do magic tricks that will include the children in the performance. Participation is a key to success, so try for at least a simple trick or two.

6. Tell a Ghost Story—The lights are low. The witches, wizards, and goblins are strangely quiet. Now is the time to tell a ghost story. Make up your own, or read one to the children. See the source list for suggestions.

7. The Old Witch Is Dead—This is a perfect party finale. Everyone sits in a circle on the floor. The leader announces, "The old witch is dead." The person on the leader's left asks, "How did she die?" The leader answers by naming some gesture or facial expression, such as "With her left arm high," holding his left arm high. Then the second player says, "The old witch is dead." The child on his or her left asks, "How did she die?" And the second child can say, "With her left arm high and a closed left eye," holding his or her left arm high and closing his or her left eye. Each new gesture is added to the last until every child has had a turn. Now the leader will say that the last gesture is so hard that he will ask everyone to answer at the same time. He will repeat the entire poem, and when everyone asks, "How did she die?" he will say, with much gusto and the appropriate gesture, "Waving goodbye!" Have the children repeat the last gesture all together.

PRIZES

Noisemakers, Play-doh, Halloween accessories like sheriff's badges and whistles.

M · E · N · U

Chocolate Spiders
Mystic Punch
Tuna Spooks
Goblin Glop
    (orange Jell-O)

AGES 6-12

Today's black cat is as likely to be a cuddly, smiling kitten, or a magical spirit radiating mystical powers, as a frightening creature with a menacing brow and an arched angry back.

Invite your guests to come as cats. Suggest a cartoon cat such as Heathcliff, Garfield, or the Pink Panther, or an individual creation like a magic cat, a baseball cat, a super-cat, a tiger or lion, a studious cat, a jeweled cat, a one-eyed cat—the list can be as long as your imagination. For those guests who want to dress up as something else on Halloween, ask them to bring something that is feline, such as a stuffed toy cat or cat food.

A cat party is perfect for fans of the musical *Cats*, adapted from T.S. Eliot's classic, *Old Possum's Book of Practical Cats*. What better time to have a Jellicle Ball than on Halloween? Invite your guests to come dressed as one of the cats from the book or the play—from Macavity, the Mystery Cat, to Old Deuteronomy or the Railway Cat.

INVITATION

For the Cat Party, the obvious invitation will still work: a cutout of a black cat with the copy written in silver or white ink. Add "eye" stickers with moving pupils for the cat's face. A tail cut out of black paper and sticking slightly out of the envelope flap will look as if the tail got stuck when you sealed the invitation.

You might also add a small rubber mouse from a toy store to the black cat invitation. Tie it to the cat's tail with orange ribbon, and mail in a padded envelope.

Some of the best invitations we have seen have been cartoon composites. The only skills required are cutting, pasting, and photocopying. Add your own message in the "balloon."

Come for a Feline Festival
Dress as your favorite cat
OCTOBER 31ST at 6:30 pm
at 21 Mulhouse Road

R.S.V.P. 555-4567

Make a Halloween tablecloth, either with your child or at the party with all the guests. Using a white paper tablecloth, decorate with sponges dipped in tempera acrylic paint, markers, stickers, and/or Halloween cutouts.

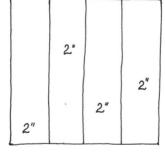

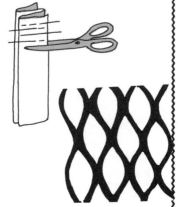

DECORATIONS

Turn your house into feline heaven:

1. Have your guests enter through a "cat door." Let them crawl through a play tunnel just inside the front door. Attach an old quilt or blanket to the top of the doorjamb, placing the tunnel entrance directly below. You will have an instant cat door.

2. Paste whiskers made of pipe cleaners onto black paper plates and hang from the ceiling.

3. On black and orange balloons, with felt-tip markers, draw eyes (or use eye stickers) and whiskers.

4. Hang black crepe paper cobwebs everywhere. To make: open a sheet of black crepe paper. Beginning at one side, fold over 2 inches. Continue folding over until the entire sheet is folded. It will measure 2 inches by whatever the length of the paper is (usually 20 inches). Make a cut on one folded side, about 1¾ inches long. Do *not* cut all the way to the other side. Stop about ¼ inch from the edge. Now flip the paper over and make another cut, beginning on the opposite side of the paper—and ¼ inch from your last cut. Again, do not cut all the way through—the closer together you make the cuts, the lacier the web.

Continue cutting and flipping until the entire length of the crepe paper is cut. Now gently shake it all out. Hang the paper with fishing line or tape, or drape over chairs, cabinets, tables, and doors.

5. Find a picture of a black cat with a distinct outline shape or use ours. Photocopy the picture and then have it enlarged at a copy facility. Using the enlargement as your guide, cut out as many cats as possible and place them everywhere—against the walls, pasted on broomsticks, hanging from the ceiling, flat on the table, and taped on doors and windows.

6. Gather old white pillowcases and hang as ghosts. Stuff the closed end of each case with fabric or newspaper (or simply insert rubber balls), tie below the stuffing to form a head, and let them hang down. You can draw two black eyes on each pillowcase. String them up by attaching fishing line or heavy twine through the top of the head.

7. Pull black yarn throughout the party room, over and under and through the furniture and doors, leaving enough room for the cats to play safely. Every now and then, leave some small balls of yarn hanging for the "kittens."

8. It will be easy to find accessories with cats on them: paper plates and cups, tablecloths, cards, mugs, lanterns, masks, and posters. All stuffed animal cats should come out for the night. A cat with a couple of balls of yarn and a tiny rubber mouse next to it will make a clever centerpiece for the dining room table.

9. When distributing or serving Halloween candy, refer to it as "cat food" or "cat nibbles."

ACTIVITIES

1. The Witch's Cat—Before the party, make up a silly or scary tale involving "the nine lives of the witch's cat," who has just died. In his memory, have the children sit in a circle on the floor in a darkened room, all holding the edge of a large blanket in their left hands so it balloons out in front of them and covers the floor. As you describe each of the nine lives, place an object, representing a part of the dead cat, under the blanket. These objects should only be felt, never seen, by the children, who will pass them to one another with their right hands under the blanket. As each object is passed from hand to hand, the witch announces which part of the cat it is and continues with her spine-tingling tale. The story can be embellished by members of the group. You will need:

- a piece of fur—the cat's skin
- a mushy grape—his eye
- a pickle—his tongue
- a set of false plastic teeth
- a ball of yarn—his head
- a short feather boa—his tail
- a bowl of cooked wet macaroni—his guts
- plastic press-on nails—his claws
- pieces of straw from a broom—his whiskers

In Charleston, Massachusetts, Maggie Moss Tucker and the neighbors in her block association get together to make Halloween fun for the whole neighborhood. They have even enlisted the Tufts University Marching Band, whose members come in full costumes, to parade through the town. Halloween has become Charleston's most popular celebration.

Why did the witch cross the road?
It was the chicken's day off!

39

2. The Cat Got Your Tongue—Use all or part of the following list. Adapt the entries for your age group. Give each player paper and pencil. The first game is to list words beginning with "cat." You give the clues and the one who gets the most words wins.

CLUE	ANSWER
1. Underground caverns for burying	catacombs
2. A large church	cathedral
3. Before he was a butterfly he was a	caterpillar
4. A book you can order things from	catalog
5. A growth in your eye	cataract
6. If I throw a baseball, you should	catch it
7. Cows, bulls, and steer	cattle
8. A sailboat with two hulls	catamaran
9. A Christian religion	Catholicism
10. A terrible tragedy	catastrophe
11. It flies but meows like a cat	catbird
12. A thief that climbs outside houses	cat burglar
13. A section of things that are alike	category
14. It swims	catfish
15. A red mushy tomato sauce	catsup

Another version has the players naming parts of a cat:

CLUE	ANSWER
1. A story	tale (tail)
2. Part of a needle	eye
3. Front lights of a car	head
4. What a barber shaves	whiskers
5. Parts of a saw	teeth
6. A kind of tree	fir (fur)
7. If you stop for a second	pause (paws)
8. A part of a sentence	clause (claws)

Joshua Mann, from Santa Barbara, tapes a funny message for his trick or treating friends on his videotape. He then sets up the television by the window, and when the bell rings, he starts the tape and his film debut is there for all to see.

3. Prowling for Cats—Hide cats made of candy or paper cutouts all over the house. The children will search for the cats' "nine lives." The player who collects nine cats first is the winner. Or you can have many winners by having prizes for the biggest cat found, the smallest, the weirdest, the brightest, and so on.

4. Name the Cat's Nose—Draw a simple cat's face on an old sheet. Cut a small hole in the center of the face just large enough for a nose to go through. The sheet should be suspended from the ceiling, so position the cat face an appropriate distance from the top and bottom. Divide the children into two teams. One team hides behind the sheet as, one by one (or several at a time if you have drawn more than one face on the sheet), the players stick their noses through the hole. The other team will try to guess the identity of each nose.

5. Doughnut Race—String doughnuts on a heavy cord all the way across the room. Use enough doughnuts so each player has at least one. At a signal, the players will reach up with their mouths, hands behind their backs, and eat the doughnuts. The trick is not to bite into the hole (because it will then fall off the cord). Prizes are given for the players who finish without dropping the doughnut.

6. Ball of Tricks—Unwind a ball of black yarn. Write some instructions to perform silly tricks ("sing a song," "jump up and down on one foot," "do ten pushups") on small pieces of paper and punch a hole in each piece of paper. Tie a trick to the yarn every 2 feet or so. Wind the yarn up into a big ball. If the papers show, you can add more yarn to the ball. Now seat the players in a circle. The first player will unwind the yarn until he comes to the first paper. He will read it aloud and follow the instructions. Then he will throw the ball of yarn to someone else in the circle. Continue until all the guests have performed.

When Peter Gaulke was four, he dressed up as a crayon for trick or treating. His treat? He gave out crayons to each person who gave him a treat.

If a cat jumps in your lap, good luck is coming.

PRIZES

T.S. Eliot's *Old Possum's Book of Practical Cats*, a paperback published by Harcourt Brace Jovanovich, is a wonderful prize for winning games at any Cat Party. The cassette tape from the musical *Cats* is always a big hit. There are other books about cats for all ages (see Sources section). A small stuffed animal cat, cat stickers, a cat mask, or a mug with a cat on it are all welcome prizes.

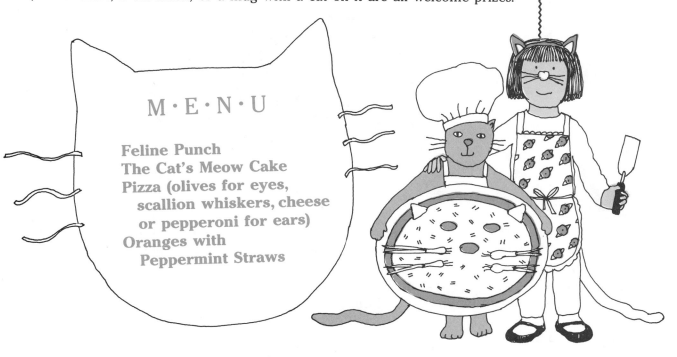

M·E·N·U

Feline Punch
The Cat's Meow Cake
Pizza (olives for eyes,
    scallion whiskers, cheese
    or pepperoni for ears)
Oranges with
    Peppermint Straws

MONSTER MASH

AGES 6–12

Monsters, witches, vampires, ghosts, and goblins—everything macabre, gory, grotesque, and just plain weird makes Halloween the "monstrous" holiday everybody loves and no one wants to miss.

Glorifying the grisly doesn't mean we cannot make light of it. The Monster Mash makes the gruesome whimsical and amusing, and works especially well for young revelers.

INVITATION

Buy inexpensive paper eye masks at a stationery, party, or toy store. Write the invitation copy on the back side (which is usually white).

Why does the mummy keep his Band-Aids in the freezer?
He uses them for cold cuts.

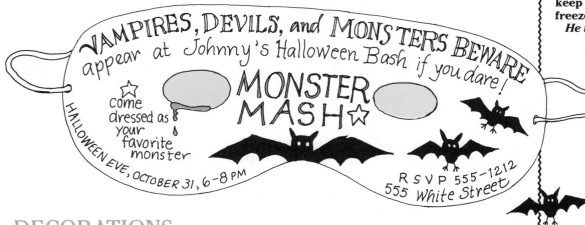

DECORATIONS

1. Bats everywhere! Bats are easy to cut out of black construction paper or black felt. Have them hanging in bunches in as many corners as you can. Spread spider webs (see page 38) around the room. Hang paper skeletons, vampires, and witches. Cover the table with a paper cloth and place rubber spiders and insects all over the table.

2. Cover the front door with black crepe paper. Cut out white paper teeth and glue them in the form of an open mouth. Glue red crepe-paper drops as if blood is dripping from the mouth.

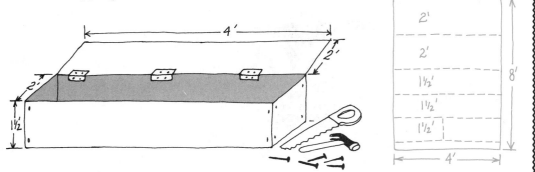

3. Make a coffin out of one sheet of 4-foot by 8-foot pressboard. Cut and nail together. Make a door with hinges and put a handle on one side so the kids can open the coffin. Have a live person (one of your helpers) lie down inside, dressed in full gory costume, including mask, paws, and/or monster makeup. He will sit up every time the coffin door is opened. A cardboard coffin-making kit is also available at Halloween time, from Hallmark stores.

4. Play spooky sound-effects tapes continuously. Check your local record store; they usually carry special horror tapes and records in the month before Halloween. A Gilbar favorite is a series of recordings called *Horror Rock Classics,*

At John McKiernan's toy store in Mamaroneck, New York, it has become a tradition that at the end of the day on Halloween, friends and customers come back to the store to celebrate with caldrons of dry ice, mirrored balls with spotlights, black lights, and all animated store displays in motion. John's favorite trick is to wear a costume within a costume. Last year he wore a black felt executioner's hood; after sporting that for a while, he peeled off a layer to reveal an old-man costume.

Volumes I and II—the records are cut out in the shape of a bat and a pumpkin, and include songs like "The Monster Mash," "The Blob," "Twilight Zone," and "Cemetery Girls." Volume I has another old favorite: "The Purple People Eater." They also publish *Elvira's Haunted Hits,* on record and tape, which has other ghostly favorites, including the theme from *Ghostbusters.* If you cannot find them at your record store, you can order them directly from Rhino Records (see Sources section).

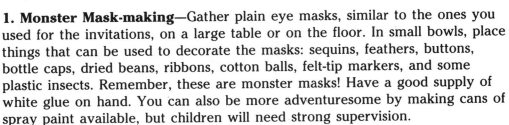

ACTIVITIES

1. Monster Mask-making—Gather plain eye masks, similar to the ones you used for the invitations, on a large table or on the floor. In small bowls, place things that can be used to decorate the masks: sequins, feathers, buttons, bottle caps, dried beans, ribbons, cotton balls, felt-tip markers, and some plastic insects. Remember, these are monster masks! Have a good supply of white glue on hand. You can also be more adventuresome by making cans of spray paint available, but children will need strong supervision.

Another version of mask-making entails creating masks from plaster. Kits can be purchased (Make a Mask kits are available from Penny Whistle Toys all year round), or you can work from scratch. The resulting mask will be fabulous:

• Buy a roll of Plaster of Paris bandages (made by Johnson & Johnson, available at pharmacies). You will need one roll per mask to create a strong surface. Cut into 2-inch lengths.

• Grease the face well with Vaseline.

• Dip the strips into a bowl of water, one by one, and squeeze all water out before applying to the face.

• Repeat strip by strip, overlapping strips by about ½ inch. Smooth out the strips as you go. Leave breathing holes and eye openings.

• The entire process of application takes 10 to 12 minutes from Vaseline application to peeling off the mask. The mask will actually separate from the face as it dries.

• In another 15 to 20 minutes, the mask is ready to be painted with acrylic paints.

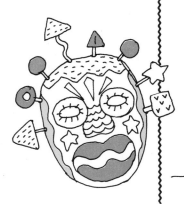

2. Make Your Own Monster—Remind the children that Frankenstein, the King of Monsters, was created from parts of people's bodies. Now they can make their own monsters from "home bodies"—things found around the house. Collect boxes—cereal, cardboard, toothpaste, soap, detergent, and so on—cardboard tubes and cones, and any other household leftovers you can glue together. We have also used miniature plastic hangers, paper nail files, plastic bottle caps, empty spray cans, empty adhesive tape dispensers, and paper clips. Gather the children in an open area where they can create their own monsters by gluing and taping these items together (with packing tape).

3. The Monster Dash—Divide the guest monsters into two teams and line them up in two rows at one end of the room. At the other end of the room, put two small empty pans, bowls, or plates on a table. Hand an apple and a spatula to the first person at the head of each team. Beside each team place a bowl of "monster teeth" (dried white beans). When you yell, "Monsters dash!" the first person on each team puts some of the "teeth" on his spatula, the apple on his head, and walks to the other side of the room. He drops the "teeth" into the team's bowl and returns to his team, with the apple still on his head. He then transfers the apple and spatula to the next person in line on his team. The team that finishes first wins.

4. Halloween Word Search—Kids love the challenge of a word search. Use words that have to do with monsters and Halloween. This activity is especially handy when the party needs to be toned down a notch. Photocopy this list or make up your own to hand out to the children. Give them a certain amount of time to find the words, depending on their ages.

If you sing before breakfast, you'll cry before dinner.

```
T U R W B P L U O H G V S G
S R V I L M A G I C O U P T
O W I T U X W D T U B S O A
H S Q C A T I R V H L E O B
G B T H K P Z V A A I N K D
P N W Y B O A S M L N O Y F
R O S T X N R Q P L R T R M
C T M R A C D T I O Q S D O
O E A A L M O P R W S B O N
S L S P I D E R E E K M O S
T E K E B M O T N E A O L T
U K H I C A N D Y N J T B E
M S P U M P K I N F O B S R
E P I T A P H M S C A R E D
```

Words:

Halloween	vampire
pumpkin	trick or treat
ghost	spooky
ghoul	cat
witch	mask
wizard	epitaph
magic	candy
skeleton	party
scared	blood
tombstone	monster
spider	goblin
costume	

45

Is it true that witches aren't afraid of dead bodies?
Of corpse!

5. Monster Mash—Time to dance! In a darkened room, with fast music playing, watch those monsters frolic. Buy a small gadget called a "flasher button" at your local hardware store to insert into the light socket. It will make the lights flicker continuously and spookily. To make it even more fun, give one guest monster a witch's broom or a cardboard skeleton with moving parts. He has to dance with that broom and pass it to someone else as he is dancing. The object is to keep the broom passing from dancer to dancer because, when the music stops, whoever is left holding the broom is out of the competition.

6. The Shadow Movie—Arrange the stage before the party. Stretch a cord high across one end of the room and hang a bed sheet on it. Guests will sit in rows in front of the sheet to make an audience. Behind the sheet, place a lamp with a single bulb so it can throw shadows on the sheet from anyone standing behind it. When the play is ready, you will act it out behind the sheet and the audience will see only shadows. This can be a silent film (with no sounds from the players) or a talking movie. Make sure you have some immediately identifiable props like chairs, a table, and whatever you will need for your star performer.

Here is an example of a story you can perform in a shadow movie: "The Witch Doctor." An old witch with a long nose is standing behind the sheet, wearing a pointed hat and a robe—these sharp images will cast terrific shadows—stirring a liquid in a large pot with a long spoon. She is mumbling various incantations over the obviously boiling pot. There is a knock at the door. A boy enters, moaning, groaning, and complaining about stomach pains. The witch gives him some brew that puts him to sleep on the table. Wielding a huge cardboard knife, the witch pretends to cut open his stomach. She then reaches in and removes a series of objects—a coil of rope, an eggbeater, a shoe, an alarm clock (which you can pre-set to ring), a bottle, a hat, and so on. These objects are simply lying flat behind the boy but from in front of the sheet they look like they are coming out of his stomach. The witch mutters and cackles to herself, making funny comments about the stuff that is coming out.

After the operation is over, the witch sews up the patient, using a huge needle and thread, which is really a pencil with a rope tied to it. Then she wakes the boy up and asks him if he feels better. He says he feels great, pays the witch, and exits to great hoots from the audience.

7. Murder—This is a game you play with a deck of cards, using as many cards as there are players. You always use the ace of hearts and the 2 of clubs. Shuffle the cards and have each person draw one card. Players do not tell anyone what card they have. Tell everyone that the guest holding the ace of hearts is the murderer (no one else knows who he is), and the one with the 2 of clubs is the attorney (everyone can know his identity). The attorney then turns off the light, which leaves the room totally dark, and he leaves. Everybody moves about, including the murderer.

While the players are moving, the murderer chooses a victim, whom he grabs very gently by the neck. The person who is grabbed must scream and fall to the floor. As soon as the attorney hears the scream, he immediately returns and turns on the light. Everybody freezes and the attorney instructs the court to come to order. The attorney can question anybody he wants to: everybody except the murderer must answer truthfully, and the murderer must lie. The attorney can figure out who the murderer is by asking obvious questions (what color shoes are you wearing?). If someone tells the truth, he knows that person is not the murderer. The game ends when the attorney guesses the murderer. The game can then be repeated.

PRIZES

Stores that sell Halloween costumes and props are usually well supplied with a multitude of "pick-up" items that will be suitable prizes. Look for skeleton key chains, spider rings, fake vampire blood, horns, and makeup.

Aspen has adopted Halloween as its own "national" holiday. The town goes all out—there is even an unwritten rule that anyone entering Aspen on Halloween Day must be in costume. The result is that everyone, from shopkeepers to ski instructors to bus drivers and even babies in strollers, is seen in their imagination's best.

WHEN YOUR RAZOR IS DULL, AND YOU WANT TO SHAVE, THINK OF THE MAN THAT LIES IN THIS GRAVE.

M·E·N·U

Devil Dogs with Blood and Skeleton Fries
Vampire Punch
Nightcrawlers
Monster Mash Mess
(red Jello-O with strawberries)

NIGHTMARE ON MAPLE STREET

AGES 12 AND FOREVER

Your guests will never forget this party. From the time they receive their invitations to the moment they leave the haunted house you have created, the atmosphere is so enveloping that everyone will instantly get into the Halloween spirit. Soon they will be swearing that they hear the dead sending messages, feel ghosts on their shoulders, and see phantom apparitions in odd corners. And they will be right! Add the activities and music and food, and this party will have everybody talking.

INVITATION

To set the mood for this unforgettably spooky party, our first choice for the invitation is a drawing of a haunted house (see below). Photocopy this drawing in black and white, and color the front door red or orange. The front of the invitation reads "Nightmare on Maple Street." Write the invitation copy on the back.

The invitation could also be a tombstone. Write an amusing epitaph on one side of a brown sandwich bag, incorporating your guest's name: "Here lies the body of James Atkinson Terrier, who burst while drinking his morning Perrier," "Here lies Paul Carter, father of 29, there would have been more, but he didn't have time!" and so on. On the other side use the same copy as the haunted house invitation.

DECORATIONS

You cannot overdo the decorations for this party. The more spider webs, plastic insects, phony tombstones, hanging ghosts, balloons, witches, and bats, the better. This is your chance to "overdecorate" your house, basement, or party room. The aim is to turn your home into a phantom-filled, ghoulish horror that will delight your guests.

If you have a front yard:

1. Place black or white candles inside carved-out pumpkins (cut with faces of ghouls), up the front walk and/or stairs. The eerie effect of candlelight is

Use Fleck Stone spray paint and acrylic topcoat to give your "tombstones" the look of real stone.

* Ariana Gordon starts collecting old dolls from her friends a few weeks before Halloween. Dolls with missing limbs are particularly popular, because the dolls are half-buried in Ariana's front yard on Halloween night. When her friends arrive for her annual party, they make tombstones with silly sayings and set them around the Doll Cemetery. Dad's scattered spotlights around the yard help maintain the illusion of a graveyard.

perfect for Halloween. But please be aware of the potential danger that candles can pose, especially when placed in areas where children are marching around in their often voluminous costumes. If this is a concern for you, just use small flashlights in the pumpkins or in plastic lanterns. You can also use all-white Christmas lights outside, although the effect will be more festive than haunted.

2. Hang ghosts made from white pillowcases (two black eyes can be added with a felt-tip marker) from trees, fences, or lampposts. Let them hang loosely so they look like they are floating. You can also use pulleys attached to the gutters of your house and have someone pull the ghosts up and down. If you can, aim outdoor spotlights at the trees to make the ghosts look eerier.

3. White balloons with black eyes drawn on them are very effective when hung in bunches.

4. Ask your florist to save dead or dying unsold flowers and wreaths that would ordinarily be thrown away. They should look straggly. Place them at the front door. If you have old Christmas wreaths that have seen better days, spray them with black paint and use them as well.

5. At the front door you can place some sort of "apparition." Create a "headless heathen" by stuffing some old clothes with rags or newspapers and placing them in a lifelike position on an old rocker or chair. Remember—no head.

Another effective spooky greeter is a plastic, rubber, or paper skeleton. Some have moving parts and will sway with the draft every time the door is opened. He may need to be spotlit.

How about a mummy? Borrow a large doll from a child (or use a mannequin) and wrap it tightly in toilet paper. Put your mummy in a homemade coffin (see page 43), or you can convert a large cardboard box painted black into a coffin. Place it outside the front door, or just inside, so that guests encounter it as they step into the house.

6. What's a haunted house without tombs? Use Styrofoam sheets, which you will find in art-supply or large party stores. Cut the Styrofoam in the shape of tombstones, and with a thick black marker write individual epitaphs on each one. Stick them into the ground at different angles with wood dowels. Again, make sure there is some dim light around so they will be visible.

7. Buy some dry ice. You can find it listed in your local Yellow Pages, under Dry Ice. Buy it the morning of the party because it will not last more than a day in your freezer. That evening, put the ice pieces in a large bucket and place in a spot that is out of the way, preferably on a raised shelf, so any rambunctious guests will not bump into it and get hurt. Do not touch the ice with your bare hands. Use rubber gloves to handle it and keep it safely out of the way of small children.

That's just the outside. Now do not disappoint them inside.

1. Music sets the scene instantly. There are several cassette tapes you can buy. Card shops, paper-goods stores, and many toy stores carry Halloween mood tapes in the weeks preceding the holiday. Some are also available throughout the year in record and tape stores (see Sources section).

2. Set decorators will tell you that the best and easiest trick to create instant atmosphere is to use colored lights—so change all the light bulbs to blue.

3. Candles are excellent mood setters but can be a fire hazard. Use them only in attended areas. If you do use them, try using only black and white candles. Cluster them in bunches on the dining room table and on other raised and flat surfaces.

4. You will need spider webs everywhere. The more the room is covered with them, the spookier it will look. You can make them (see page 38) or buy sacks of webs, made especially for decoration, and spread them in batches all around the house. To be effective the webs should be bunched together. You can also augment the feeling by tying black or white string or yarn around the house, anchoring it on various pieces of furniture. Make sure it serves as decoration, not as a barrier to sitting or moving around. You can also buy cheesecloth at grocery or fabric stores and strew it about. At Halloween you will find unusual objects at magic stores. Our favorite is a battery-operated hand that can be placed on a table, in a corner, or on top of a "grave" site. It will move for hours. These hands seem to hold people spellbound, especially if you find the right setting.

5. Your dining room table, decorated to the hilt, will serve as the centerpiece for the room. People will gravitate to it naturally. That is where the food is, but they should also be entertained by what is on it. First cover the table with a solid-colored cloth (paper or plastic will do). Place spider webs and tiny plastic or rubber insects all over it (they seem to be readily available at toy or party-goods stores during this time of the year). A group of small pumpkins with eyes shining, from the votive candles inside them, will look great scattered about or clustered in the center of the table.

Place your trick or treat goodies inside a coffin. Let the kids lift the lid and get the candy themselves.

Marian and Howard Downs had a Nightmare on California Street party, full of playfulness and invention, at their Victorian home in San Francisco. The decorations were outstanding: wilted funeral sprays on tripods all along the front walk and stairs; tombstones perched on mounds of dirt in the front yard; mannequins sawed in half, placed in the bathroom tub and sink; a skeleton under covers in their bed, holding a breakfast tray with moldy food; and a real coffin harboring a fully dressed mannequin to greet the guests at the front door.

An added variation: If your guests will be seated for dinner, cover the back of each chair with a large brown bag, supermarket size, complete with an epitaph. Write each guest's name on the "tombstone."

For a bizarre attraction, rent or buy a mannequin from a supply house. Dress her in an old wedding dress. Attach 30-pound clear plastic fishing line around the limbs and waist and hang her from the ceiling, until she is about 2 feet above the dining room table. Your levitating bride could even eliminate the need for a centerpiece.

6. At various places around the house, hang the following with clear fishing line: black bats; black top hats; ghosts made from pillowcases; skeletons; and mummies, which can be made by wrapping toilet paper around your children's dolls. Any bathroom used by your guests can display oddities or ghoulishness. Use your imagination. For example, have a pair of doll legs positioned so they look like they are going down the drain.

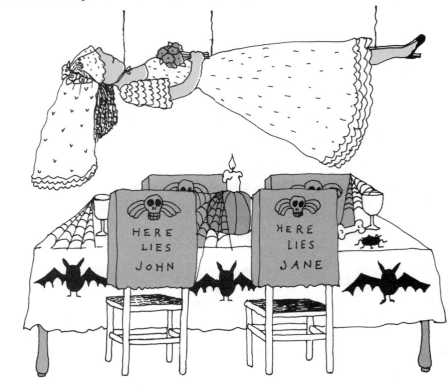

ACTIVITIES

1. Fortunetelling—Hire at least one fortuneteller to be stationed at a booth so each guest can have an individual session, or you can have a helper play the fortuneteller. If you do, before the party, cut out horoscopes from monthly magazines. They are longer and more detailed than the daily horoscopes you find in newspapers. Keep them under wraps so your guests think the "fortuneteller" is really "seeing the future." Be inventive in creating a crystal ball out of a glass fish bowl or a round vase turned upside down. Magic 8 Balls are yet another possibility.

You can also read fortunes from playing cards. Have one of your helpers memorize the following cards and fortunes, or have the guidelines hidden under a napkin while he is reading the cards. For more information on fortunetelling from playing cards, you can get a book called *Fortune Telling with Cards,* by P. Foli.

An apple peel thrown over your left shoulder will curl up into the initial of the one you love.

Hearts:	KING:	You will be a famous rock star.
	QUEEN:	You will be President.
	ACE:	You will have your own airplane.
	TEN:	You are funny and will be a famous comedian.
	NINE:	You will be powerful and kind to many people and own your own basketball team.
	SIX:	You are not tall now but you will be taller than your parents.
Clubs:	KING:	You will own many McDonald's restaurants.
	QUEEN:	You will be a doctor who cures many people.
	ACE:	You are stubborn and will be very successful.
	TEN:	People will write to you from all over the world because you will be a newspaper reporter.
	EIGHT:	You will design famous homes and live in one.
	SEVEN:	You will travel to the moon.
Diamonds:	KING:	You will be very rich and will give lots of money away to people who need it.
	QUEEN:	You will have a silver Ferrari and race it all over the world.
	ACE:	You will be a famous baseball player.

2. A Seance—Hold a seance, preferably in a small room. This is a great activity for a small group. If it is a large party, hold seances for a few guests at a time. For decor, replace the light bulbs with colored ones, which will give the room an unearthly look. Draw the curtains and pull the shades to create a feeling of intimacy. Candlelight enhances the atmosphere. The Ouija board is the center of attraction here. Have the guests sit on the floor around a coffee table that has been covered with a dark cloth.

You can hire a "medium" or find a friend who would like the challenge of acting as one. Those who know about such things say that mediums often have auras of light around them. You get this effect by putting some strips of iridescent tape on the medium's clothing.

The medium takes immediate control of the seance. He or she addresses the guests and "spirits" in the room and leads the seance, following the instructions that come with the Ouija board game.

J.J. Ramberg, from Los Angeles, makes a cardboard robot with tube arms through which the Rambergs send out trick or treat candy.

3. Dancing—An ultimate icebreaker and something that can go on during the entire party. This is a party where all the activities and events should be happening simultaneously. Dancing should be in one room, food in another, and the fortuneteller holds forth in her own space. With your guests moving freely from area to area, this party plan makes the role of host very easy!

4. Magic Show—Magicians can be fun for all ages. Amateur magicians may be your best bet because they bring great enthusiasm to the job. Don't forget—Johnny Carson started as one.

5. Scavenger Hunt—For a teenage crowd, a scavenger hunt is always a big hit. Type out a list of items that have something to do with Halloween or the occult. Some suggestions include:

lock of hair	piece of white cloth
foreign coin	red pen
pumpkin seed	piece of black yarn
bones	dead flowers
the date from today's newspaper	epitaph
torn photograph	candy wrappers
makeup brush	anything orange
picture of a witch	black hat

Give each guest a trick or treat bag and send them out in groups. Set a reasonable time limit—say, half an hour—and have prizes ready for the team that returns with the most items on the list.

PRIZES

A tape of Halloween sound effects, a book of Edgar Allan Poe's poems, or a magic trick all make good prizes.

Author Bud Trillin's favorite holiday is Halloween. Luckily he lives in Greenwich Village, New York, site of the annual Halloween People's Parade. The tradition was started in 1976 by Broadway costume designer Ralph Lee, who wanted to showcase his extravagant ornamental costumes and masks. From a small, neighborhood parade, where Lee's actor, mime, and dancer friends marched, it has now become an enormous event, aided by grants from the National Endowment for the Arts, with thousands of fully costumed revelers marching every year. A recent favorite was a group of teachers who came as Imelda Marcos' shoes. The Trillins build their annual Halloween party around the parade, inviting their guests to march and then over to their home for Halloween treats.

M·E·N·U

Choco Lanterns
Roasted Pumpkin Seeds
Mulled Cider
Gingerbread Ghosts
Quesadillas
Guacamole and Chips
Ham Rolls with Mustard Sauce

HOUSE TO HOUSE HAPPENING

AGES 12 AND FOREVER

Here's how to trick or treat for those, twelve and up, whose days of trick or treating are numbered or over, but who do not want to admit it. The guests at this party will visit four homes for a progressive four-course dinner (one dish at each home) and will trick and treat in each. The guests will walk or travel from one home or apartment to another, spending about 30 to 45 minutes in each.

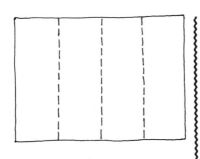

INVITATION

Take a sheet of legal-size paper (8½ inches by 13 inches). Fold over across the 13-inch side once, and then fold it again. You now have a folded sheet of paper, 8½ inches by 3¼ inches. Copy the house drawing shown here on one panel of the paper. Cut along the solid lines of the drawing. When done, open up and you have a series of four identical attached houses. You can copy the verses below or make up your own.

The Hermans'   555 Bowing Place   6:00 P.M. sharp
Dress: Halloween

Your first stop for this Halloween Happening is here,
You're lucky to start at our place,
An appetizer will wet your desire for more,
But watch out for the tricks you must face!

The Rogers'   666 Huntington Drive   6:45 P.M.

Your second great dish of the feast is awaitin'
As is a great Halloween game,
So hurry on through all the tricks at the Hermans
Or you'll miss all the treats, what a shame!

The Meyers'   888 Buckley Street   7:30 P.M.

So far it's been lovely, we venture to say,
You're probably having a ball,
But your third dish for dinner is sitting around
Just waiting for you all to call!

The Browns'   444 Fourth Avenue   8:15 P.M.

And now you are coming to the last stop tonight,
To have your dessert (it's not small!),
But more tricks and games do await you, you know,
It's Halloween night, after all!

RSVP 555-8615

DECORATIONS

Each family will decorate their house using their own creative style, which will make each a little different, even if they all decide on the haunted-house theme. Tombstones, spider webs, a levitating mannequin, creepy crawlers on the tables, skeletons in corners, and jack-o'-lanterns everywhere will do it well.

One of the houses might be turned into a pumpkin patch. Carve and light pumpkins all over the house. Decorate with cornstalks, leaves, and haystacks. Make a pumpkin diorama (see page 15) for a centerpiece.

Sometimes it is easiest to choose one or more Halloween images—cats, witches, bats—and carry the theme throughout the house. Bats can fly from the ceiling, hover over chairs and sofas, and cover the table. Create a witch by pinning or taping a black cape on a wall. Attach a witch's hat above it. A plastic caldron with dry ice (see page 51) directly beneath the witch will complete the effect. And if you want to invest more, there are battery- and electric-powered moving witches, Draculas, and ghosts that will surely wake up the dead.

Another option is to decorate the house in one chosen color. Light the room with colored lights. Color all bats and witches the same. Devise a menu with foods in that color.

ACTIVITIES

1. House No. 1—Have a covered box with a hand-sized hole in its top inside the front entrance. As each guest arrives, he sticks a hand inside the box to identify its contents. You can provide a pencil and paper and have each person identify as many things as he can. Objects in the box can include: a dog biscuit, a dried fig, Silly Putty, an eraser, an ear of dried corn, a coin, a spoon, a ball of yarn or string, a candle, a feather, a sock, a hair clip, and a walnut. If you are braver, you can add peeled grapes and warn your guests to watch out for eyeballs! A prize should be given to the person who correctly identifies the most items.

Always wear something red at Halloween—ghosts are afraid of it!

When the guests are done and while they are eating their appetizer, give them a sheet of paper and ask them to unscramble words about Halloween. You may want to use this sample:

HTOSG	ghost
HUGLO	ghoul
NIOBLG	goblin
IRKTC	trick
ATETR	treat
YARCS	scary
NLALEWHEO	Halloween
HTWCI	witch
PPKMUNI	pumpkin
RURSCAETE	creatures
NHUDEAT	haunted
RVAYDEARG	graveyard
KOLEETNS	skeleton
DPSISRE	spiders
SORENTM	monster

What do you get when you cross Dracula and Sleeping Beauty?
Tired blood.

Be prepared for the unexpected:
• Have extra food and drinks, favors, props, and light bulbs.
• Have a fire extinguisher in working order and in the house, especially if you are using candles for decoration.
• Have a complete medical kit at hand.

2. House No. 2—Halloween Hallucinations—This is a variation on charades. Assign each guest the name of a famous person or a character associated with Halloween. Taking turns, the "hallucinator" mimes the characteristics of the person he is supposed to be. The others can call out their guesses. This can be played by teams as well.

3. House No. 3—Food Games
• Apple Chase: Have apples hanging from the ceiling (by tying strings to their stems). The trick is to bite into the apple, eating it without letting it drop from the string.
• Marshmallow Swallow: Divide the guests into pairs. Give each couple a string about 2 feet long with a marshmallow strung in the middle of it. Each person in the pair puts an end of the string in his or her mouth. When the "go" is given, each person begins to chew the string. Whoever gets to the marshmallow first, wins!

4. House No. 4—Dictionary Draw—This host will need a large pad of white paper, a black marking pen with a wide tip, and an easel. On slips of paper, write words that have something to do with Halloween. Some choices:

Put the slips of paper in a hat or a plastic pumpkin. Divide the guests into two teams. A player on the first team begins by picking a slip of paper, keeping the word to himself, and drawing what it means on a large pad of paper held on an easel. Only the members of his own team can guess. They have 1 or 2 minutes. A timer is helpful. If they guess correctly, they get 100 points and another person on that team gets to go up. If they do not guess correctly, it is the other team's turn. The team with the most points wins.

5. Since this is the end of the evening, you may want to have music going and suggest dancing or a musical game such as freeze dancing. You can use any of the music listed in our Sources section.

PRIZES

Halloween candy.

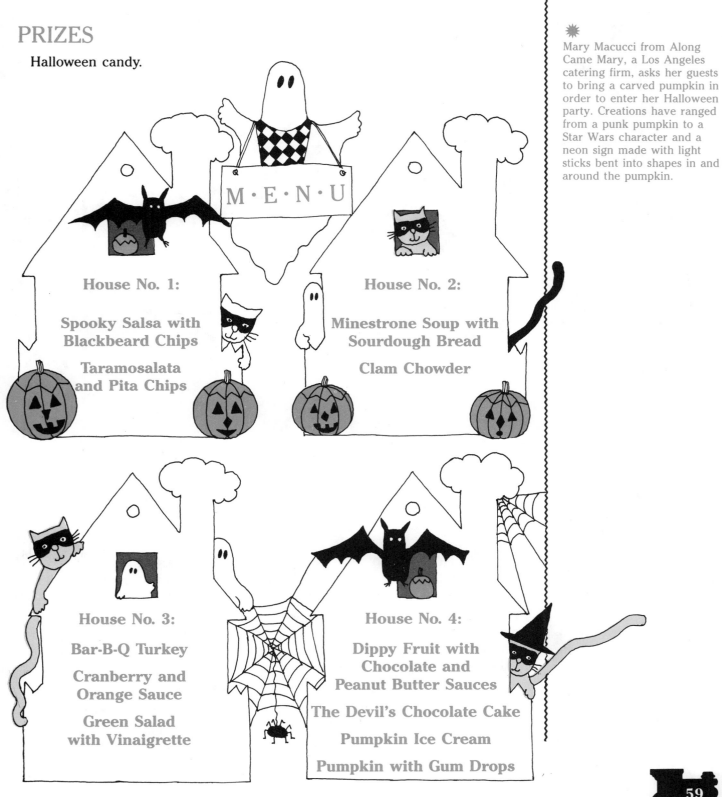

House No. 1:

Spooky Salsa with Blackbeard Chips

Taramosalata and Pita Chips

House No. 2:

Minestrone Soup with Sourdough Bread

Clam Chowder

House No. 3:

Bar-B-Q Turkey

Cranberry and Orange Sauce

Green Salad with Vinaigrette

House No. 4:

Dippy Fruit with Chocolate and Peanut Butter Sauces

The Devil's Chocolate Cake

Pumpkin Ice Cream

Pumpkin with Gum Drops

✳ Mary Macucci from Along Came Mary, a Los Angeles catering firm, asks her guests to bring a carved pumpkin in order to enter her Halloween party. Creations have ranged from a punk pumpkin to a Star Wars character and a neon sign made with light sticks bent into shapes in and around the pumpkin.

CARNIVAL

ALL AGES

Winning a goldfish at the Throw a Ping-Pong in the Goldfish Bowl Booth, dunking a fully clothed classmate in the Revenge on Your Friends Booth, or getting all those cans to fall with one throw of the baseball at the Casey at the Bat Arcade are familiar challenges and fun to replicate at home. Expand or pare down the festival depending on your space, the number of guests you have invited, and your energy level. The Carnival works for all ages and can be adapted for a house or yard. The activities include booths that are set up ahead of time and games of skill that operate continuously and can be played at any time during the festivities.

Have plenty of adults on hand to assist. You will need them to oversee the activities with you.

INVITATION

Our first choice is a ghost invitation, as seen at right. You can copy ours or make your own version. To carry out the ghost theme, you will be making BOO coupons to give out at the party, as described below.

Tracy Zabar, from New York, one of the readers of *The Penny Whistle Party Planner*, sent us another suggestion: take close-up Polaroid pictures of your child or children in funny poses or in a costume. You will want six photos in total. Place the photos in two rows of three so they fill up an 8½-inch by 11-inch sheet of paper. Write the invitation copy along the bottom of each photo, then photocopy the completed invitation to make as many duplicates as you need. A sample:

Together with your children, color around the images or fill in the faces with crayons or markers. Mail in a colored envelope that is 10 inches by 12 inches so the invitation lies flat with no folds.

DECORATIONS & ACTIVITIES

At this party we have combined the decorations and activities sections because they are so intertwined.

Cut out lots of "BOO" coupons in the shape of little ghosts, as in the invitation. These will be given out every time a guest wins at a booth and redeemed at the "Carnival Store" at the end of the festivities.

Set up the garage or parts of rooms as booths at the carnival.

1. Bluebeard's Castle—A Chamber of Horrors. The garage is the perfect place, although a basement will do as well. If the room is not already dark, hang black sheets or dark paper tablecloths on the walls and over any windows. Hang rags down from the ceiling. You can buy strips of fabric at most paint stores if your rag bag is empty. They should fall at different levels so that some will reach a guest's waist while others will touch his face. Strings suspended from the ceiling will feel like cobwebs. You can have a fan blowing all the hanging elements. Place thick foam rubber mats on the floor in various locations.

61

Have a one-color party. Everyone is invited to come in whatever costume he or she wants, as long as it is all in the chosen color.

This is the ideal spot to have haunted-house sounds in the background. You can buy ready-made recordings (see Sources section) or sound effects. Select helpers to be in charge of dropping a heavy book, rubbing a wet finger around the rim of a glass of water next to the victim's ear, rattling some chains together, and shaking empty tin cans in a bucket. Use your imagination to create unusual sounds. Test them while keeping your eyes closed; many ordinary sounds are magnified and seem eerie when you cannot see what is making them.

You will need a guide, Bluebeard, to lead each blindfolded victim through his castle. As each guest walks through, he experiences many weird and spooky phenomena. The first encounter is with Bluebeard's late wives' body parts.

- Take one or more rubber kitchen gloves, fill with water, and freeze. Hang the frozen gloves from a string and have Bluebeard urge the victim to shake the hands of the deceased.
- Have a bowl of peeled grapes so your guest will think he is feeling eyeballs.
- A bowl of cooked wet spaghetti will feel like "guts." A bowl of cooked oatmeal can be brains, and nutshells can be toenails.
- A piece of fake fur or an old wig can be the late wives' hair.

Next, Bluebeard will lead his victim to walk the plank, our version of a favorite old-fashioned game in which kids feel like they are going to fall. Two henchmen will aid him in this deed. You will need a board, approximately 8 inches wide by 3 feet long, placed on top of two bricks (so it balances like a seesaw). The victim will be guided to step up on the board, in the middle, and told he must walk the plank. Bluebeard stands in front of the victim and holds his hands at all times. A henchman is at each end of the board to hold it steady, with the victim standing on the board in between. The henchmen will pretend to lift the board very high, but this will be an illusion. Bluebeard will sink down to his knees, still holding the victim's hands up high—this gives the victim the sensation of being lifted into the air. Bluebeard tells his victim that when he lets go of his hands, the victim must jump into the sea. The victim then jumps, only to find, to his surprise, that he is just a few inches off the ground.

At the end of the horror at Bluebeard's, give each survivor one BOO coupon—or more if he has been particularly brave or if you are feeling generous.

2. Apple Bobbing Booth—This is a Halloween classic, and like most classics, it has withstood the test of time and still works well for all ages. This tradition actually started with the Druids, when apples were considered to have mystical powers. Those who won at apple bobbing were assured of good fortune the rest of the year.

You need a plastic tub on the kitchen table filled with water and bobbing apples. Each person, with his hands behind his back, must reach down to bite an apple and remove it from the water. Whoever can bring up an apple gets a BOO coupon.

3. Future Darts—Get a Velcro dart board—it should have Velcro balls and numbers on the board—and attach it to a wall. On a piece of paper, write some funny and strange fortunes that correspond to the numbers on the board. Whenever a player hits a number, read his or her fortune. Each player gets three tries, and three fortunes. When he is done throwing the balls, reward him with a BOO coupon for every 10 points amassed.

4. Pumpkin Toss—Carve out several pumpkins of varied sizes and line them up in a row. Paint a number on each: 5, 10, 15, and 20—that will be the point system. The object is to stand behind a line and throw whole, unshelled walnuts into the pumpkins to get the largest total of points possible. Award BOO coupons to all players according to their point totals. For example, you can give one coupon for every 5 points. You can also devise your own award system.

5. Get the Cat Out of the Well—Decorate a large cardboard box with a paper tablecloth with a Halloween design. Fill with cutouts of black cats, each with a paper clip attached to it. Make fishing poles by tying pieces of 3-foot-long string about 3 inches from the end of 3-foot-long wooden dowels. Attach a magnet to the other end of each string. Divide the players into two teams. Without looking into the box, one player from each team has 30 seconds to fish for the cats (there are two players fishing at the same time). The team with the most cats wins.

6. Photo Stop—Set up a booth using a Polaroid camera. Appoint someone as the official photographer so the portrait-taking becomes a formal affair. For kids dressed in full Halloween regalia, it is fun to take home a picture of themselves ready for the scrapbook.

Joey Slamon, age six, makes Halloween place mats every Halloween. Together with her mom, Obie, they collect stickers and cut out appropriate images from magazines. As the kids arrive for Joey's party, they each make a place mat, gluing the cutouts and stickers onto a piece of construction paper. When they are done, Obie covers each with transparent contact paper. The kids then get to eat on the place mats they have made.

Never rock an empty rocker—it's bad luck!

Barbara Harvey Branden-burgh went to a Halloween scavenger hunt in Tulsa, Oklahoma. Instead of bringing back actual articles, each team had to return with Polaroid pictures of the items on the list. Therefore, things on the list could include people, like the town's mayor; animals, like a black cat; and objects, like the clock at the bank.

7. Peter, Peter, the Pumpkin Reader—Pumpkin seeds are the medium from which Peter reads fortunes. Peter can be dressed as a pumpkin or a fortune-teller. Take thirty pumpkin seeds and, with a felt-tip pen, write the numbers 1 through 10, three times, which will give you three sets of numbered pumpkin seeds.

Put them in a glass bowl. The guest will pick three seeds without looking and will then hand them to Peter, who will tell the three fortunes, one from each number. Peter may be very clever and can make up his own fortunes, or he can follow these suggestions. But remember, Peter should be prepared to embellish.

1=You will find great wealth.
2=You will be a star.
3=You will have many children.
4=Your chances of winning the lottery are great this week.
5=You are inquisitive; you will be a reporter.
6=You will be a great doctor or nurse.
7=You will be an important and famous writer.
8=You will be a great actor in the theater.
9=You will score the winning goal in a soccer game.
10=You will be a great explorer and find a treasure.

PRIZES

Instead of just awarding prizes for winning, set up a Carnival Store as one of your booths. Have small prizes lined up on a table, each with a price in front of it—the guests will trade in their BOO coupons for prizes, depending on how many they won. Examples: skeleton or rabbit's foot key chains can be bought for 5 coupons while Silly Putty will cost 10 coupons.

Carol Chalmers, owner of the Toy Store in Sun Valley, Idaho, says the best costumes are found in your closet. One year she found enough stuff in her closet to be Goldilocks and the Three Bears—the only thing she had to buy was snouts!

M·E·N·U

Perfect Popcorn Balls
Candied Apples
Orange Popsicles
Mysterious Doughnuts
Bobbing Apple Punch
Make-Your-Own Taco Bar

BARNYARD BASH

PUMPKIN BREAD

⅓ cup vegetable oil
½ teaspoon ground cloves
1 cup fresh or canned pumpkin purée
3 eggs
1 cup sugar
2 teaspoons ground cinnamon
½ cup raisins
2⅓ cups Bisquick
Pinch of ground nutmeg (optional)

Preheat the oven to 350 degrees. Grease a 9- by 5-inch loaf pan.

In a large bowl, mix all the ingredients together with a wooden spoon. Pour the mixture into the prepared pan. Bake for 45 minutes. Test with a knife—if the knife comes out clean, the bread is ready. If not, put it back in the oven for another 5 to 10 minutes. Cool before removing from the pan. Keep in a plastic bag, in a covered dish on the counter or in the refrigerator.

When you are ready to serve, cut out slices with a pumpkin-shaped cookie cutter and spread with cream cheese or jam.

SERVES 12 TO 18

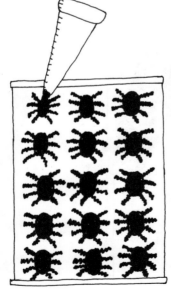

SUGAR COOKIE PUMPKINS

1 cup butter or margarine, softened
1 cup sugar
3 eggs
1 teaspoon vanilla
3 cups all-purpose flour
½ teaspoon baking soda
½ teaspoon baking powder
1 cookie decorator (in a 4½-ounce pressurized can)

In a large bowl with an electric mixer, blend together the butter and sugar. Add the eggs, vanilla, and 1 cup flour and mix well. By hand, fold in the remaining flour, the baking soda, and the baking powder. Refrigerate for at least 2 hours.

Preheat the oven to 375 degrees. Lightly grease a large baking sheet.

On a lightly floured board, roll out the dough until it is ⅛ inch thick. Cut out the cookies with a pumpkin cookie cutter and place on the baking sheet. Bake for 8 to 10 minutes, until lightly browned. Remove from the oven and let cool thoroughly on a wire rack before decorating.

MAKES 2 TO 3 DOZEN COOKIES

WITCHES, WIZARDS, AND GOBLINS GANG

CHOCOLATE SPIDERS

4 cups semisweet chocolate baking chips

In the top of a double boiler, over simmering water, stir the chocolate chips until they melt. Remove from heat. Let stand over the water until the chocolate is cool but still fluid, about 10 minutes.

Take our drawing of a spider and photocopy or draw again on a piece of paper, making as many as will fit about 1 inch apart on a legal-size piece of paper (or cut a piece 12 inches by 15 inches, which is the size of a baking sheet). You now have a sheet of paper with lots of spiders drawn on it. Place this paper on the baking sheet and cover with a sheet of wax paper.

Pour the chocolate into a pastry bag that has been fitted with a ⅛-inch or ¼-inch tip. Fold the top edge to seal. Squeeze the chocolate out of the pastry bag onto the wax paper, tracing the pattern of the spiders. If the chocolate is runny, it needs to be cooled a little longer. If you have leftover chocolate when you are done with this sheet, move the pattern onto another baking sheet, cover with wax paper, and start again.

Chill the spiders for about 10 minutes. When they are hard, they can be peeled off the paper. You can store them in the refrigerator, laid flat on a cookie sheet or plate. If you layer them, separate the layers with wax paper.

You can use the spiders to decorate a table or hand them out to the kids. Our children enjoy putting them on their tongues, closing their mouths, and then talking to unsuspecting guests. When they open their mouths—there are the spiders! Make at least 3 to 4 per child—they disappear fast.

MAKES ABOUT 4 DOZEN SPIDERS

MYSTIC PUNCH

Ice cubes with raisins frozen in
    them to look like "insects"
4 1-pint bottles cranberry juice
2½ cups juice from 2 1-pound,
    14-ounce cans of spiced peaches
1 cup fresh lime juice (about 8 limes)
2 cups orange juice
    Sugar to taste

Keep the juices refrigerated until you are ready to use them. In a punch bowl, combine all the juices. Add the ice cubes and serve.

MAKES 20 CUPS

TUNA SPOOKS

2 8-ounce cans white tuna,
    packed in water
3 tablespoons mayonnaise or
    plain yogurt
1 8-ounce can water chestnuts, sliced
½ teaspoon curry powder
1 tablespoon honey mustard
20 slices wheat bread, crusts removed
    Whipped cream cheese
    Black olive slices for garnish

Mix the tuna, mayonnaise, water chestnuts, curry powder, and mustard in a medium bowl. Cut the bread slices with a cookie cutter in the shape of gingerbread men. Spread 10 slices with the tuna mixture and cover each with a second slice of bread.

Now spread the top of each "spook" with cream cheese. Use two slices of olive to make eyes on each.

MAKES 10

CATS

FELINE PUNCH

2 1-quart bottles cranberry-apple
    drink
1 cup brown sugar
1 1-quart bottle ginger ale
2 whole oranges
    Whole cloves

Heat the cranberry-apple drink and sugar in a pan until the sugar is dissolved. Let cool thoroughly. When ready to serve, pour into a punch bowl and add the ginger ale.

Create faces on the oranges by studding them with whole cloves to form eyes, noses, and mouths. Place in the punch. Add ice cubes just before serving.

MAKES 24 ½-cup servings

THE CAT'S MEOW CAKE

Also known as "Grandma Tillie Buhai's Ice Box Cake," this treat has been a favorite at the Buhai households for the last four generations. This adaptation will delight your guests.

12 eggs
5 bars sweet chocolate
2 tablespoons water
4 packages ladyfingers

In two bowls, separate the eggs. In a glass bowl, melt the chocolate bars together with the water in a microwave. Add the unbeaten egg yolks to the melted chocolate and immediately stir until smooth. Let cool.

In another bowl, beat the egg whites until stiff and fold into the cooled chocolate mixture.

Line the bottom and sides of a 12-inch springform pan with split ladyfingers (be sure to cut the bottom of the ladyfingers so they will stand better). Use small pieces to fill in the spaces on the bottom of the pan. Now pour one-third of the chocolate mixture over the ladyfingers

Joyce Bogart puts dry ice in a large bowl and sets her smaller punch bowl inside. She buys the dry ice that afternoon (it lasts only 6 to 8 hours), chops it up into several smaller pieces, and puts it in the bowl using tongs.

67

on the botton and add some ladyfingers on top of the chocolate. Continue layering, ending with chocolate on the top layer. Refrigerate overnight and keep cold until you are ready to serve. Top with the Whipped Cream.

SERVES 12 TO 16

WHIPPED CREAM:
  ½ *pint heavy cream*
  ¼ *cup sugar*
  1 *tablespoon vanilla*

Beat the cream until thick. Add the sugar and vanilla and mix well. Spread on the cake to cover the top (you will have enough to cover the sides as well, if you like).

You can decorate the cake with black jelly beans for the eyes and nose, and chocolate-covered mint sticks for whiskers. You can also buy a cat's rubber nose (available at Halloween party stores) and place it in the center of the cake.

ORANGES WITH PEPPERMINT STRAWS
  16 *oranges*
  16 *peppermint sticks*

With an apple corer, cut into each orange about three-fourths of the way down. Insert a peppermint stick into each hole so that it fits snugly. The stick becomes the straw. Advise each child to squeeze his orange—this will make the juice go up the straw.

MAKES 16

MONSTER MASH

DEVIL DOGS WITH BLOOD AND SKELETON FRIES
Cook hot dogs as you would normally, on the stove or the grill. Take the buns and, with a scissor, cut out little triangles on the top part facing outward. When done, the bun will look like a mouth with the upper teeth showing. Place the hot dog inside, serve with blood (ketchup) and skeleton fries (French fries).

VAMPIRE PUNCH
  8 *cups cranberry juice*
  6 *cups sparkling apple cider*
  6 *orange slices*

Put all ingredients in a punch bowl. Add ice cubes just before serving.

MAKES 14 CUPS

NIGHTCRAWLERS
  12 *large apples*
  1 *8-ounce jar boysenberry jam*
  4 *tablespoons butter*
  12 *gummy worms*

Preheat the oven to 350 degrees.

Core the apples from the stem end to ½ inch from the bottom. Do not push through. Stuff each hole with 1 teaspoon each of jam and butter.

Place in a pan and bake uncovered for 35 to 45 minutes, depending on the size of the apples. When done, the apples should be tender but not mushy. Remove the apples from the oven. Let cool for 15 minutes.

Now set each apple in a bowl and spoon syrup from the baking pan around it. In the top of each apple, insert a gummy worm with at least half of its body protruding.

MAKES 12

NIGHTMARE ON MAPLE STREET

CHOCO LANTERNS
  12 *miniature pumpkins*
  1 *cup sugar*
  ⅔ *cup cocoa powder*
  4 *tablespoons cornstarch*
  ¼ *teaspoon salt*
  5 *cups milk*
  1 *teaspoon vanilla*

Cut the tops off the pumpkins and remove most of the interior with a sharp knife. Then scoop out the rest with an ice-cream scoop to even out the inside.

In a bowl, mix together the sugar, cocoa, cornstarch, and salt. Add the milk gradually as you mix with a wooden spoon. Pour into a saucepan and cook over medium heat, stirring constantly, until the pudding thickens. Now add the vanilla and mix again. Remove from the heat and pour into the hollowed-out pumpkins. Chill until ready to serve.

MAKES 12

ROASTED PUMPKIN SEEDS

   Pumpkin seeds
   Water
   Salt
   Melted butter
   Pam vegetable spray

Preheat the oven to 350 degrees.

Rinse the seeds well. For every 2 cups of seeds, put 4 cups of water and 2 tablespoons of salt into a saucepan. Add the seeds and simmer over low heat for 10 minutes. Drain well in a colander. Place on paper towels and pat dry.

Toss the pumpkin seeds with melted, unsalted butter (1 tablespoon of butter for every 2 cups of seeds) in a large bowl until the seeds are evenly coated.

Spray a roasting pan or a cookie sheet with Pam vegetable spray. Spread the pumpkin seeds over the tray and bake for 30 minutes, stirring and tossing occasionally. When the seeds are golden brown, they are ready.

If you make this the day before, store them in an airtight metal or plastic container in a cool place.

MULLED CIDER
   6 1-inch cinnamon sticks
   1 tablespoon whole cloves
   1 tablespoon whole allspice
   2 pieces whole nutmeg
   2 cups brown sugar
   1 gallon apple cider
  16 whole cinnamon sticks

Tie the first four ingredients in a cloth bag. In a large pot, stir together the sugar and the cider. Add the spice bag. Bring to a boil and simmer for about 20 minutes. Remove the spice bag and serve hot with a whole cinnamon stick in each mug.

SERVES 16

GINGERBREAD GHOSTS
   ½ cup sugar
   ½ cup butter or margarine, softened
   ⅓ cup molasses
  2½ cups sifted all-purpose flour
   2 teaspoons ground ginger
   ¾ teaspoon baking soda
   ½ teaspoon ground cinnamon
      Pinch of salt

In a large bowl, blend together the sugar and butter. Add the molasses. Fold in the sifted flour, ginger, baking soda, cinnamon, and salt. Refrigerate for at least 2 hours.

Preheat the oven to 350 degrees. Lightly grease a large baking sheet.

On a lightly floured board, roll out the dough until it is ⅛ inch thick. Cut out the cookies with a gingerbread-shaped cookie cutter and place on the baking sheet. Bake for 6 to 8 minutes, until lightly browned. Remove from the oven and let cool thoroughly on a wire rack before decorating with Frosting.

MAKES 2 DOZEN

FROSTING:
   1 16-ounce box powdered sugar
   1 teaspoon vanilla
      Pinch of salt
   3 to 4 tablespoons milk
   1 8-ounce package miniature
      chocolate chips

Take half of the sugar and add the vanilla, salt, and 2 tablespoons of the milk. Mix well. Now add the remaining sugar and mix again. Add as much of the remaining milk as you need to reach the desired consistency for spreading. Spread the Frosting on each cookie until it is totally white and looks like a ghost. For eyes, use two miniature chocolate chips on each cookie.

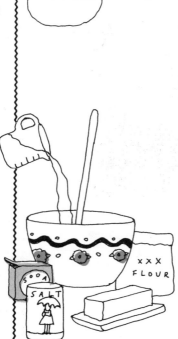

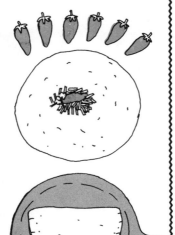

QUESADILLAS

5 jalapeño peppers, chopped
1 pound jack cheese, grated
1 cup chopped parsley
16 tortillas

Combine the peppers, cheese, and parsley. Place a portion of the mixture in the middle of a flat tortilla. Fold over and press the edges together. Spray a large skillet with Pam and fry the tortillas over medium heat, or toast in your toaster oven. The quesadilla is ready when the cheese has melted. Keep warm until ready to serve or reheat in the toaster oven for 5 minutes. Do not reheat in the microwave. You may want to make some without the peppers for those who don't like them hot.

MAKES 16

GUACAMOLE

4 ripe avocados, mashed
1 tomato, peeled and chopped
2 tablespoons finely chopped onions
2 tablespoons lemon juice
Salt and pepper to taste
Dash of Tabasco sauce

Combine all the ingredients in the food processor and mix for 15 seconds. Return the avocado seeds to the mixture to keep it from turning brown. Store covered in the refrigerator until ready to serve. Serve with taco chips (try the black ones).

MAKES 3 CUPS

HAM ROLLS WITH MUSTARD SAUCE

Buy cooked ham slices. Roll them into cylinders and serve with Mustard Sauce.

MUSTARD SAUCE:
1 cup Coleman's dry mustard
1 cup cider vinegar
1 cup sugar
3 eggs, beaten

In a saucepan, mix together the mustard and vinegar. Let sit, covered, overnight on the kitchen counter (it will cook itself—you can see it bubble). In the morning, stir in the sugar and eggs.

Cook, stirring over low heat, for 15 minutes. Store in a covered jar in the refrigerator until ready to serve.

MAKES 2 CUPS

HOUSE TO HOUSE HAPPENING

SPOOKY SALSA

1 small red pepper, seeded
and chopped
1 small yellow pepper, seeded
and chopped
1 medium onion, chopped
4 scallions, sliced
3 plum tomatoes, seeded
and chopped
2 tablespoons olive oil
1 8-ounce can tomato sauce or
8-ounce bottle chili sauce
3 tablespoons chopped fresh cilantro
1 teaspoon black pepper
Pinch of salt

In a large frying pan, sauté the peppers, onions, and tomatoes in the oil until tender, about 4 minutes. Add the tomato sauce and cilantro and cook for another 6 minutes, stirring occasionally. Add the pepper and salt and stir to blend.

This recipe can be served warm or cold, with blue corn chips, salted taco chips, or fresh vegetables.

MAKES 2 CUPS

TARAMOSALATA AND PITA CHIPS

2 slices white bread, crusts removed
4 tablespoons water
1 cup tarama (available in Greek
markets) or salmon roe caviar
1 small clove garlic, mashed
1 tablespoon finely chopped onion
3 tablespoons lemon juice
½ cup olive oil
8 pita breads

Soak the white bread in the water. Place in the food processor with all the other ingredients except the olive oil and pita breads. Blend until the mixture forms a smooth, creamy paste. Now add the olive oil, a teaspoon at a time. When the taramosalata is smooth, place in a serving bowl. Cover until ready to serve.

Cut each pita bread in half so you have two flat circles. Cut each circle in quarters. Toast the "chips" in the toaster oven and serve along side the Taramosalata.

MAKES 1½ CUPS

MINESTRONE SOUP

- ¼ cup olive oil or margarine
- 2 onions, thinly sliced
- 2 cups sliced carrots
- 2 cups peeled and diced potatoes
- 5 broccoli florets, cut up
- 4 green zucchini, sliced
- 1 bunch leeks, chopped
- 6 cups low-sodium chicken broth
- 1 16-ounce can Italian plum tomatoes, drained and cut up
- ¼ teaspoon celery salt
- 1 10-ounce package frozen spinach
- 1 15-ounce can pinto beans, drained
- 1 15-ounce can red kidney beans, drained
- 1 cup uncooked macaroni, any size
- ⅓ cup grated Parmesan cheese, optional

Heat the oil or margarine in a very large pot over medium heat. The cooking method is easy to remember—add each of the vegetables, in turn, and cook each for 3 to 4 minutes. Start with the onions and cook until soft. Now add the carrots and cook; then add the potatoes, broccoli, zucchini, and leeks in turn. Next, add the chicken broth, tomatoes, and celery salt, and let the whole concoction cook over a low flame for an hour. Now add the spinach, still frozen, and cook for 10 minutes. Add the beans and macaroni, and cook for another 10 minutes. If you find the soup getting too thick, add a cup of water. When done, cool before refrigerating. Reheat to serve, and top with Parmesan cheese, if desired.

MAKES 10 BOWLS OR 18 TO 20 MUG SERVINGS

CLAM CHOWDER

- 1½ cups water
- 3 8-ounce cans minced clams, liquid reserved
- 3 medium potatoes, peeled and diced
- 1 medium onion, chopped
- ½ cup butter
- 1½ quarts half-and-half
  Salt and pepper to taste
- 2 tablespoons chopped parsley

Place the water and the liquid from the clams in a large saucepan and add the potatoes. Bring to a simmering boil and cook for 5 to 7 minutes. Add the onion and simmer for another 2 minutes. Now add the clams, butter, half and half, salt and pepper, and parsley and simmer gently for 30 minutes.

SERVES 8 TO 10

BAR-B-Q TURKEY

- 1 10-pound turkey (have the butcher cut it in half)
- 1 cup fresh lime juice
  Salt and pepper to taste

Place the turkey halves cut side down, skin side up on a prepared grill. Cover and cook, basting every now and then with the lime juice. After about 1 hour, sprinkle with salt and pepper. Continue to cook for another ½ hour, or until the juices run clear when the turkey is pricked with a fork.

SERVES 20

CRANBERRY AND ORANGE SAUCE

- 2 16-ounce cans whole cranberries
- 1 8-ounce can crushed pineapple
- 1 orange, with peel, cut into chunks

Put all the ingredients in a large bowl and mix with a wooden spoon. Serve at room temperature.

MAKES 4 CUPS

VINAIGRETTE FOR GREEN SALAD

    6   tablespoons good-quality olive oil
    2   tablespoons vinegar or lemon juice
    2   cloves garlic, mashed
    1   teaspoon Dijon mustard
    1   teaspoon dried basil or 2 teaspoons
        chopped fresh basil
    ¼   teaspoon salt and pepper to taste

Put the oil and vinegar in a glass bowl and whisk. Add all the other ingredients, letting the garlic swim in the dressing until just ready to pour on the salad.

MAKES ½ CUP

DIPPY FRUIT

Serve sliced apples, pears, bananas, and whole strawberries with Chocolate Sauce and Peanut Butter Sauce for dipping.

CHOCOLATE SAUCE:
    1   12-ounce package chocolate chips
    ¼   cup sugar
    1   teaspoon vanilla

Melt the chocolate chips in the top of a double boiler over simmering water. Stir until smooth. Add the sugar and vanilla, and mix well. Keep warm until ready to serve.

PEANUT BUTTER SAUCE:
    1   12-ounce package peanut butter
        chips
    2   tablespoons butter

In the top of a double boiler over simmering water, combine the peanut butter chips with the butter. Let melt and mix well. Keep warm until ready to serve.

This recipe makes ½ to ¾ cup of each sauce. If you are having a lot of guests, double the ingredients.

THE DEVIL'S CHOCOLATE CAKE

    2½ cups cake flour
    ½   cup unsweetened cocoa powder
    2   teaspoons baking soda
    ¾   teaspoon salt
    1   cup butter, at room temperature
    2¼ cups sugar
    1   teaspoon instant espresso
    2   eggs
    1   teaspoon vanilla
    2   cups buttermilk

Preheat the oven to 350 degrees. Butter a 9- by 13-inch baking pan.

In a small bowl combine the flour, cocoa, baking soda, and salt. Cream the butter in the bowl of an electric mixer or food processor. Gradually add the sugar and espresso, beating until smooth and light. Beat in the eggs, one at a time, until well mixed. Add the vanilla. Now alternate, adding the dry ingredients and milk, beating just until smooth.

Pour into the prepared pan and bake for 30 minutes, or until a knife inserted in the center comes out clean. Let cool in the pan for about 10 minutes. When thoroughly cooled, cover with Chocolate Frosting.

SERVES 12 TO 16

CHOCOLATE FROSTING:
    2   tablespoons butter
    2   ounces unsweetened chocolate
    2   tablespoons warm water
    2   teaspoons vanilla
    2   cups sifted powdered sugar

Melt the butter and chocolate in the top of a double boiler over simmering water. Add the water and vanilla, and mix. Remove from the heat and whisk in the powdered sugar until the frosting is smooth.

Spread over the cake when it is cool.

PUMPKIN ICE CREAM
  1 can pumpkin pie filling
  1 cup heavy cream
1¼ cups simple syrup (1 part water to
      1 part sugar)
  ¼ teaspoon ground cloves
  ¼ teaspoon ground ginger
  ¼ teaspoon ground cinnamon

In a bowl, mix together all of the ingredients. Pour the mixture into an electric ice-cream maker. Freeze for 20 minutes, or follow the instructions for your ice-cream machine.

MAKES 1 QUART (4 CUPS)

PUMPKIN WITH GUM DROPS
Get a large pumpkin and 2 pounds of gum drops. Place a toothpick halfway into each gum drop and stick into the pumpkin. Continue until the pumpkin is covered and looks like one mass of gum drops. Makes a superb centerpiece.

CARNIVAL

PERFECT POPCORN BALLS
(from Jolly Time, P.O. Box 178, Sioux City, Iowa 51102)

2½ quarts popped popcorn
  1 14-ounce package light caramels
  ¼ cup light corn syrup
  2 tablespoons water

Keep the popped corn warm in a 200-degree oven.

Melt the caramels in the top of a double boiler over simmering water. Add the corn syrup and water and mix until smooth. Slowly pour over the popcorn in a large bowl or pan. Stir to mix well. With greased hands, shape the mixture into balls about the size of softballs.

Let the balls cool and dry completely before wrapping (you can make them the day before). Wrap in plastic wrap or in corsage bags, available at any florist, and tie with orange and black ribbons.

MAKES ABOUT 15 BALLS

CANDIED APPLES
 12 red delicious apples
 12 wooden ice-cream sticks
4½ cups sugar
  ¾ cup light corn syrup
  1 teaspoon red food coloring
1½ cups water
  1 cup chopped peanuts

Grease a large cookie sheet and set aside.

Wash and dry the apples. Insert a stick through the stem of each, leaving about 2 inches of the stick for gripping.

In a saucepan over medium heat, combine the sugar, corn syrup, food coloring, and water. Cook, stirring constantly, until the ingredients are dissolved and the liquid boils.

Set a candy thermometer in the mixture and continue cooking, without stirring, until the temperature reaches 290 degrees, in about 20 minutes. Meanwhile, place the chopped peanuts in a bowl.

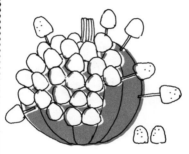

Remove the syrup from the heat and dip the apples, one by one, to coat evenly. Work quickly so the sauce doesn't harden. As you finish dipping an apple, roll it around in the peanuts to coat evenly. Then set each down on the prepared cookie sheet. Let the apples cool for at least an hour before placing on a platter to serve.

MAKES 12

ORANGE POPSICLES
Freeze orange juice in ice-cube containers with wooden ice-cream sticks. You can also freeze these in commercially available popsicle containers that come in assorted shapes.

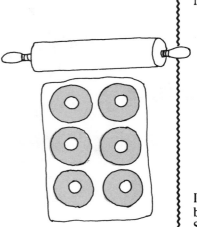

MYSTERIOUS DOUGHNUTS

    1 egg, beaten
    ½ cup brown sugar
    ¾ cup molasses
    ½ cup sour cream
    3 cups all-purpose flour
    ¾ teaspoon baking soda
    2 teaspoons baking powder
    ¾ teaspoon salt
    2 teaspoons ground ginger
      Optional toppings: powdered
        sugar, chocolate sprinkles,
        prepared frosting

In a large bowl, blend together the egg, brown sugar, molasses, and sour cream. Sift in the dry ingredients and mix well. Chill in the refrigerator for 2 to 3 hours.

Fill a large, heavy pot or an electric fryer with 4 to 5 inches of vegetable oil. Heat to 365 degrees.

On a lightly floured board, roll out the dough, a small amount at a time, until it is ½ inch thick. Cut out the doughnuts with a 3-inch floured doughnut cutter.

Fry the doughnuts for 2 to 3 minutes, or until golden brown, turning once during the cooking process.

Drain on paper towels. Now cut a small slit in each doughnut and insert a funny fortune written on a slip of paper. Sprinkle some of the doughnuts with powdered sugar or chocolate sprinkles, spread others with frosting.

MAKES ABOUT 18 DOUGHNUTS

BOBBING APPLE PUNCH

    1½ cups orange juice
     4 cups apple cider
     1 cup pineapple juice
     2 tablespoons sugar
     4 cups ginger ale, chilled
  6 to 8 small red apples
     1 orange, sliced

In a punch bowl, mix the orange juice, apple cider, pineapple juice, and sugar. Chill for a couple of hours. Just before serving, add the ginger ale, apples, orange slices, and ice cubes.

MAKES 10½ CUPS

MAKE-YOUR-OWN TACO BAR

Figure on 2 tacos per person. Use ready-made taco shells.

    4½ pounds lean ground beef or
          chicken, cooked
     4 cups shredded cheddar cheese
     3 cups chopped tomatoes
     6 cups shredded lettuce
     1 cup chopped onion
       Hot sauce
     3 cups sour cream
       Guacamole (see recipe on page 70)

Place each ingredient in a separate serving bowl with a serving spoon. Have the taco shells ready on a large platter. Each guest makes his or her own tacos, layering with the ingredients of choice.

MAKES 20 SERVINGS

SOURCES

BOOKS FOR HALLOWEEN

Ames, Lee J. *Draw Fifty Monsters, Creeps, Superheroes, Demons, Dragons, Nerds, Dirts, Ghouls, Giants, Vampires, Zombies and Other Curiosa.* Doubleday, 1986.
Black-and-white illustrations.

Barth, Edna. *Witches, Pumpkins, & Grinning Ghosts: The Story of the Halloween Symbols.* Clarion, 1981.
History of witches, paraphernalia, practices, and so on, associated with October 31.

Brown, Marc. *Arthur's Halloween.* Atlantic–Little, Brown, 1982.
Arthur the Aardvark's Halloween story; one of the Arthur series. Arthur's Halloween is about not being so frightened.

Cox, Marcia Lynn. *Make-up Monsters.* Grosset & Dunlap, N.D.

Eliot, T.S. *Old Possum's Book of Practical Cats.* Harcourt Brace Jovanovich, 1982.

Emberley, Ed. *Ed Emberley's Big Orange Drawing Book.* Little, Brown, 1980.
How-to-draw book, using simple shapes to draw Halloween pictures.

Foli, P. *Fortune Telling with Cards.* Published by McIvin Powers, Wilshire Book Company.
Contact: 12015 Sherman Road, North Hollywood, California, 91605; (213) 875-1711.

Guthrie, Donna. *The Witch Who Lives Down the Hall.* Illustrated by Amy Schwarz. Harcourt Brace Jovanovich, 1985.
A story about a little girl who is convinced that the woman who lives in the apartment down the hall is a witch.

Impey, Rosy. *The Flat Man. The Creepies Series.* Illustrated by Moira Kemp. Barrons, 1988.
A little boy hears something at the window in the middle of the night. Is it a tree limb or the flat man?

———. *Scare Yourself to Sleep. The Creepies Series.* Illustrated by Moira Kemp. Barrons, 1988.
Two little girls start to tell ghost stories and then they begin to hear noises outside their tent. (*The Creepies* are a series of scary books [for ages 6–9] told from a child's viewpoint.)

Kessel, Joyce K. *Halloween.* Carolrhoda Books, 1980.
Holiday customs are explained in this book for beginning readers.

Moseley, Keith. *The Ghosts of Creepy Castle.* Grosset & Dunlap, 1988.

———. *The Things in Mouldy Manor.* Grosset & Dunlap, 1988.
Spooky pop-ups. Every page has lots to pop up, move, and lift. (Ages 7 to 10.)

Pearson, Susan. *Porkchop's Halloween.* Illustrated by Rick Brown. Simon & Schuster, 1989.
Porkchop is Rosie's cat. Rosie is a tube of toothpaste for Halloween and Porkchop uses a pumpkin as a house. (Ages 5 to 8.)

Smith, Dick. *Dick Smith's Do-It-Yourself Monster Make-Up.* Harmony Books, 1985.

Thomas, Valerie. *Winnie the Witch.* Illustrated by J. Korky Paul. Kane-Miller Book Publishers, 1987.
British story about a witch named Winnie, who lives in a house where everything is black—including the bathtub. Winnie's cat, Wilbur, is also black, which causes Winnie some trouble.

MAIL-ORDER MAKEUP KITS

Besides the makeup kits you will find in costume shops, beauty supply stores, and toy stores around Halloween, you can also order kits and accessories from the following:

Ben Nye Company, write or call for catalog and/or direct orders, or for distribution centers in your area: 11571 Santa Monica Blvd., West Los Angeles, California 90025; (213) 477-0443.

Woochie Company, order from Columbia Stage and Screen Cosmetics, 1440 North Gower, Hollywood, California, 90028, or call Doris Butler at (213) 464-7555.

MUSIC TAPES

The following tapes can be found at your local record and tape stores and some bookstores, or you can order them from: Metacom, Inc., 1401-B West River Road North, Minneapolis, Minnesota 55411.

Mystery Superstars, Volume I includes:
  "The Shadow," Orson Welles reading "Society of the Living Dead," and "The Poison Death."
  "The Green Hornet," "Disaster Rides the Rails," and "The Ghost That Talked Too Much."
  Arch Oboler's "Lights Out Everybody," "Revolt of the Worms," and "Murder Castle."

Mystery Superstars (for older children) includes:
  "The Shadow," "The Phantom Voice," and "The Three Ghosts"—Sherlock Holmes, Alfred Hitchcock, and more.

Thriller Superstars
  "Dracula"—The Mercury Theater on-the-air production starring Orson Welles and Martin Gabel.
  "Frankenstein"/"Dr. Jekyll & Mr. Hyde"—two spine-tingling monster stories.
  "The Haunted House"—Best of Series awardwinners, "The Crawling Thing" and "Bird of Death."

The following tapes can be found in record and tape stores:

Sound Effects No. 13, "Death and Horror," BBC Cassettes, The Best of BBC TV & Radio.

Sound Effects, "Out of This World," BBC Radiophonic Workshop, BBC Cassettes.

The following tapes and records can be found in record and tape stores, or you can order them from: Rhino Records, 2225 Colorado Avenue, Santa Monica, California, 90404; (213) 828-1980.

Elvira Presents Haunted Hits, includes songs like "Ghostbusters," "The Blob," "Attack of the Killer Tomatoes," "King Kong," "Martian Hop," "Voodoo, Voodoo," and more.

Horror Rock Classics, Volumes I and II, includes songs like "Haunted House," "Purple People Eater," "Addams Family Theme," "Monster Mash," "Twilight Zone," and more. Records are shaped like bats and pumpkins.

YELLOW PAGES

Remember to use your local *Yellow Pages*—it is a superb guide to find many items you will need. Some useful headings for Halloween:

Art & Craft Supplies
Astrological Supplies and Books
Balloons
Batteries
Beads
Cake Decorating
Candy Supplies
Cheesecloth
Children's Books
Copiers
Costumes and Accessories
Dried Flowers
Dry Ice
Electrical Devices
Fabric
Fasteners
Floodlights

Grave Markers
Hardware
Lighting Accessories
Magicians
Makeup Supplies
Mannequins
Novelties
Occult Supplies
Palm Readers
Party Supplies
Plants and Nurseries
Pulleys
Records and Tapes
Toys
Trimmings
Used Clothing
Yarn

INDEX